THE BIG BOOK
OF
FAMILY GAMES

THE BIG BOOK
OF
FAMILY GAMES

The Most Complete Treasury of Fun-Filled
Games and Activities for Family and Friends

By Jerome Meyer

Hawthorn Books, Inc.   Publishers   New York

Library of Congress Catalog Card Number: 67-27334
ISBN: 0-8015-0624-7

Designed by Gene Gordon

3   4   5   6   7   8   9   10

To
Carolyn Bain,
who helped considerably
in the assembling and
editing of these games

CONTENTS

6. MAGIC TRICKS 135

7. MIND READING STUNTS 153

8. GAMES FOR THE VERY YOUNG 163

THE BIG BOOK
OF
FAMILY GAMES

WORD GAMES

ALPHABET GAME

Arrange everyone in a circle, which shall include you. Start the game off by saying the following:

"Yesterday I was at Mr. Jones' house for dinner and I had Artichokes." (Or some other edible beginning with A.)

The person sitting to the right of you now repeats what you just said, adding some edible beginning with B. For example:

"Yesterday I was at Mr. Jones' house for dinner and I had Artichokes and Beans."

The next person now repeats this, adding an edible beginning with C. For example:

"Yesterday I was at Mr. Jones' house for dinner and I had Artichokes, Beans and Cabbage."

Each person in turn repeats what the previous person has just said and adds the name of some edible beginning with the next letter in the alphabet. As the game progresses it is not necessary to say "Yesterday I was at Mr. Jones' house" each time. The players may merely start off with "I had Artichokes, Beans, Cabbage, Doughnuts, Eels, etc." but each player MUST include the entire list up to his letter (in alphabetical order) and then add his particular edible. The player who misses any of the names on the list or hesitates too long is declared out of the game. The player remaining the longest in the game wins.

ALPHABET MEMORY GAME

This is a lot of fun though it becomes quite difficult after a while and there are very few people who can complete the entire alphabet.

3

Arrange everyone in a circle, which shall include you, and start the game off by mentioning any word at all beginning with A. Suppose you say "Africa."

The person immediately to your right repeats your word, adding another word beginning with A. He may say "Africa, atlas."

The person to his right now repeats these two words and adds another word beginning with A. He may say "Africa, atlas, addition." This goes around the circle until it comes back to you. You now start off with the letter B which goes around the circle; when it comes back to you, start again with the letter C and so on.

This game is as difficult as the number of people in it. If there are ten people playing, there will be 10 A's, 10 B's, etc., so that by the time you reach the letter M you will have to remember 120 words and repeat them in the order that they are given in the game. Of course you will always hear them again and again so you will get to know them from memory, but nevertheless you have to keep your wits about you.

The player who misses any of the words is out of the game. The player who stays in the game the longest wins.

TWENTY QUESTIONS NEW STYLE

Read the following to your family or friends and bet with any one of them or all of them that they cannot guess what you have in mind in less than 35 questions. The chances are you will always win.

The thing I have in mind is neither animal, vegetable nor mineral—nor is it abstract.

It is totally useless to me yet I could not live without it. It belongs to me although nobody gave it to me and I didn't buy it, borrow it, or steal it.

I am always losing it but that doesn't worry me because it is always returned to me. If it fell off the roof of a tall building onto a hard city pavement it would not break or even crack.

Although I can see it and touch it, I can't feel it. It never makes a noise and never does any work although, on special occasions, it has been known to open things.

Dogs have it, ostriches have it too, but fish only have it in very shallow water.

(Make up a lot more things to tell your guests about this mysterious thing. *Let them ask as many questions as they like* but don't tell too much and, above all, don't mention the changeable *length* unless you want to give the thing away.)

THE THING YOU HAVE IN MIND IS YOUR SHADOW!

The photo-electric cell doors are opened by letting your shadow fall on the photo-electric cell.

TWENTY QUESTIONS—FRENCH METHOD

This is played just like Twenty Questions. Everyone is seated in a circle and the guesser stands in the center and asks each person a question in turn. All questions must have a "yes" or "no" answer and each person, of course, answers truthfully. The game is played once only and will prove to be a lot of fun for everyone except the guesser. The reason the guesser finds such difficulty in guessing the thing chosen is because it is always "the person on my right" and the guesser goes round and round, never arriving at a satisfactory answer until he sees the trick and asks, "Is it the person on your right?"

YOU DON'T KNOW WHAT YOU ARE TALKING ABOUT

Arrange everyone in a semicircle and tell them that you are going to select several speakers from among them. Each speaker is to talk for three minutes on a subject about which he knows absolutely nothing! He must keep talking on this subject and the more nonsense he talks, the better and funnier it will be for his audience who are encouraged to applaud or boo as they see fit. In case you want a few subjects to start off the game, try the following:

1. The sewer system in Moscow.
2. Duties of a tea taster's assistant in Ceylon.
3. What happens to all the pins, needles and umbrellas.
4. How many dadoes there are on the average lino and why there are not more.
5. Why seaweed is impractical for stuffing upholstery.

The winner of this game is the one who, by popular vote, talks the most foolishness. Make up your own subjects.

STUMP ORATORY

This game is very like YOU DON'T KNOW WHAT YOU ARE TALKING ABOUT except that the topics are more abstract and often inspire even loonier orations. The same rules apply. Here are a few topics as suggestions:

a. And after all, if so, why not?
b. It is and it isn't depending on whether it is or not!
c. Why we seldom say "always" and why we never say "maybe."
d. Is it colder in winter than it is in the city?

KATE'S GAME

This is a contest having to do entirely with Kate. Read the following nine questions to everyone and have them supply the correct word:

1. What Kate is always repeating? (Duplicate)
2. What Kate is always eliminating? (Eradicate)

3. What Kate is always making speeches at ceremonials? (Dedicate)
4. What Kate makes the wheels go round? (Lubricate)
5. What Kate is full of advice? (Advocate)
6. What Kate does not go around with lowbrows? (Educate)
7. What Kate is always out of breath? (Suffocate)
8. What Kate crawls out of difficult situations? (Extricate)
9. What two Kates show the way? (Locate and Indicate)

JUST TO MAKE CONVERSATION

This is one of the funniest games in the book and is sure to produce a deluge of laughter every time it is played. Select a man and a girl from your guests and tell them that they are going to hold a conversation together. Now tell them to leave the room and while they are out agree on two sentences which shall be *as opposite as possible*. One of these will be given to the man who must repeat it *word for word* in his conversation with the girl, without her noticing it. The other will be given to the girl who much repeat it *word for word* in her conversation with the man, without his noticing it. Of course neither one knows what the other's sentence is, yet they are both on the lookout for something unusual. Whoever gets away with his sentence without the other knowing it wins.

Here is a typical pair of sentences:

Mr. Smith's sentence: The sabbath is the golden clasp that binds together the volume of the week.

Miss Jones' sentence: Pickling beets in Hongkong is not as easy as you think it is.

When the conversation starts, Mr. Smith will constantly be leading Miss Jones into religious subjects until he can put over his little sentence unnoticed by Miss Jones. Miss Jones, on the other hand will try to take Mr. Smith with her to China where she can introduce the pickling of beets and get off her sentence unnoticed by Mr. Smith.

Here are a few suggestions for other sentences:

> Boy's sentence: Never show an ostrich that you are afraid of him.
> Girl's sentence: I always fry everything in lard.

> Boy's sentence: They say that one should feed a cold and starve a fever.
> Girl's sentence: Einstein was the world's greatest scientist.

POOR PUSSY

This is an old but very amusing game and never fails to create shrieks of laughter.

Line up the guests so that the girls face the boys. The lines should be about six feet apart. The first boy in line starts by going over to the first girl, kneeling in front of her and saying "meow" three times. The girl must stroke the boy's head each time he says "meow" and say "Poor Pussy" without smiling. If the girl does this successfully in spite of the laughter from the rest of the guests, she goes over to the next boy in line kneels and says "meow" three times. This time the boy must stroke the girl's head and say "Poor Pussy" just as before.

The game continues until some serious minded winner has been able to keep a straight face each time his turn came.

GHOSTS

Divide everyone into two equal parts or sides and let them sit facing one another. Make a man the "captain" of side 1 and a girl the "captain" of side 2. The man begins the game with a letter—any letter that comes into his head. Suppose it is K. The girl then adds another letter with the idea of starting a word which someone else has to finish. She might say N, having in mind the word "Knot." Now the next person on the opposite (man's) side adds a letter. He may say I instead of O with the word "Knife" in mind. This goes on from one side to the other until a word is spelled and the person who adds the completing letter to the word is declared "out" once. If he is out three times he is a ghost and nobody must talk to him although he may talk to everyone and try to get them to talk to him. Anyone who talks to a "ghost" becomes one himself.

GHOSTS IN MODERN DRESS

This game is ideal for small groups. It is played like the old game of Ghosts. Instead of using letters we shall use pairs of words in such a manner that the *first word of one pair becomes the last word of the next pair* and the pairs string along.

There are thousands of words in the English language that are commonly associated with other words, for example: love letter, note paper, price war, dance hall, cry baby, water fall, etc. These can be connected to other pairs of commonly associated words *when the last word of one pair becomes the first word of the succeeding pair* and, if the last word in the next pair becomes the first word in the following pair, we can have a regular string of pairs of words.

Let us take a few for example:

1. lunch box—box spring—spring time—time lock—lock up—
2. red hot—hot dog—dog collar—collar button—button hook—
3. side car—car rail—rail way—way back—back hand—hand out—

Start a player off with some common pair of words to which he must attach another common pair of words, the first word of *his* pair to be the last word of *your* pair. The next player must attach another common pair of words to his pair and so on until someone gets stuck and can't go on. Anyone who can't continue is out and must start a new pair going. If he is out three times he is a streamlined ghost and nobody may talk to him.

Here is a typical game: You start the game with "back up" (or any other pair).

1st PLAYER: "Up town."

2nd PLAYER: "Town folk."

3rd PLAYER: "Folk song."

4th PLAYER: "Song writing."

5th PLAYER: "Writing paper."

6th PLAYER: (*out to stump the next fellow*): "Paper money."

7th PLAYER (*undisturbed*):"Money back."

8th PLAYER: "Back out."

9th PLAYER: "Out wit."

10th PLAYER: "I can't continue. I can't think of a pair that starts with wit. My new pair is: full house."

Number 10 is out once and the game starts all over with the new pair, "full house," and continues until someone can't go on.

WRONG IS RIGHT

Form two lines, one of girls and the other of boys. Have them stand up and face one another. The object of this game is to answer questions incorrectly; anyone giving the correct answer must sit down.

The boy at the head of the line starts by asking the girl opposite him a question. She must answer immediately and if she answers that question correctly she must sit down and be declared out of the game. If she gives the wrong answer she must ask the next boy in line (the second boy) another question and he, after answering it wrong, asks the girl opposite him another question—and so on down the line and back again. The winner is the one who remains standing the longest. The answers to all questions must be immediate—any hesitation puts a player out of the game.

ENDLESS CHAIN OF CITIES

Arrange the players in a circle, which shall include you, and let anyone start by naming an American city beginning with A. Suppose he says "Albany." Albany ends in Y so the next person must name a city beginning with Y. Suppose he says "Youngstown." Youngstown ends in N so the next person must name a city beginning with N and so on. All answers must be immediate and anyone hesitating or failing to follow in the regular order is declared out of the game.

THE MOULTING OSTRICH

Arrange all the players in a circle and appoint a leader who is to smile sweetly and say in low voice to each·player in turn:

"My poor ostrich is moulting and I don't know what to do!"

Without laughing or smiling each player suggests what to do for the poor moulting ostrich. If anyone laughs or smiles during this procedure, he or she is immediately eliminated from the game.

Of course the leader tries to make the players smile and the more ridiculous he acts the better it will be. If he succeeds in going the rounds without everyone being eliminated for smiling, he is to add to his first statement and start all over again. The second statement is as follows:

"My poor ostrich is moulting and I don't know what to do because I happen to be anemic."

Of course the winner will be the one who remains longest in the game. He or she should be booed for being the biggest grouch!

SPEED READING

Select two or three paragraphs from any newspaper. Any paragraphs will do. The object of this game is to read these paragraphs in the shortest possible time—the host or hostess being the official time-keeper. The winner will be the one who, without laughing, reads the selection clearly and distinctly in the shortest possible time.

In case there are ties or the game is too easy, the following introduction to *Spelling Bees* by Albert Deane is to be read distinctly in the shortest possible time:

"The infectious proclivity for polysyllabic interchange of incomprehensible and occasionally irrefutable and unanswerable ratiocination, invective and oftentimes laryngeal trivialities is a poltroonery that is permissible of the most censorious and punitive retaliation. To possess an aggrandized vocabulary is a mental endowment transcending the encyclopedical attributes of pedagogues who must investigate, peruse and burrow for the scintillating segments of verisimilitude normally secreted from those whose knowledge is enchorial and whose verbiage is enclitic.

"Exuberant and exultant propensities in phraseology continually lead to cerebral extradition for malefactors guilty of philological pyrotechnics. Perspicacious pundits scrupulously shun irreverent behaviorism and invariably take innocent refuge in the incontestable sanctuary of benign blandiloquence. Or by way of antithetical alternative, in mundane myopia.

"Malicious malingerers in the realm of obsequious vacuity intermittently and agonizingly bewail the punctiliousness of those superlatively heirloomed with the gifts of psychic penetration. To their pettifogging mentalities any laboriously contrived device so minutely registering a mechanism as a micromotoscope would loom gargantuan by invidious comparison. To elucidate for the benefit of such individuals would parallel the espousal of eudemonics by Italo-Ethiopian esthetes. One unmitigated and undisputed contention is that philological parsimoniousness is particularly preferable to loquacious laxity, especially as demonstrated by evanescent nincompoops of the lower cerebral classification."

I AM THINKING OF A NAME

This is without doubt one of the most fascinating games ever devised. While it is ideal for the parlor, it is a mighty powerful entertainer and time-killer on trains, auto trips, boats or any other place where small groups gather and want to pass the time.

One person, whom we shall call the leader for want of a better name, thinks of the name of a famous person—either alive or dead—and announces the initial of his or her last name to the rest of the players. Suppose he chooses William S. Gilbert, the famous English humorist and playwright. He announces the following:

"I am thinking of a person whose last name begins with G."

It is then up to the players to find out what the name of that person is in the shortest time and under the following rules:

1. Players may ask as many questions as they like and at any time they want to.
2. All questions must be specific and refer *only to the occupation or vocation* of a person whose name begins with the given letter.
3. The leader must answer all questions truthfully by mentioning some other person fitting the occupation mentioned in the question and beginning with the required initial (in this case G).
4. If the leader fails to think of a person fitting the occupation or vocation and beginning with the required intitial, the questioner may ask one leading question. He may ask: "Is he living or dead?" or "Is it a man or a woman?" or "Is he a European or an American?" etc.
5. Every time the leader fails in his answer, another leading question may be asked and the questioner may always be challenged by the leader.
6. Once the status of the person is determined the players must adhere strictly to that status and ask questions only in con-

nection with it. For example, if by leading questions it is found that the unknown person is dead and a European, only quesions about dead Europeans must be asked.

Here is a typical game in detail: The person is William S. Gilbert.

LEADER: "I am thinking of a person whose last name begins with G."

PLAYER: "Was he a great Hindu and a lawyer?"

LEADER: "No, it is not Gandhi."

PLAYER: "Was he an English king?"

LEADER: "No, it is not George."

PLAYER: "Was he a composer?"

LEADER: "No, it is not Gershwin."

PLAYER (out to stump the leader): "Was he an artist who did something phenomenal?"

LEADER (not being able to recall any great artist whose last name begins with G and who did something phenomenal): "I give up and challenge you."

PLAYER: "The name is Giotto and my leading question is: is this person alive or dead?"

LEADER: "Dead."

(From now on all questions must refer to a *dead* person whose last name begins with G.)

PLAYER: "Was he ever President of the United States?"

LEADER: "No, it was not Grant."

PLAYER (out for the leader's scalp): "Was he an Italian patriot?"

LEADER (unable to think of a dead Italian patriot whose last name began with G, submits and challenges the questioner).

PLAYER: "The name is Garibaldi and my leading question is: is he an American or a European?"

LEADER: "A European."

(From now on all questions must refer to a *dead European* whose last name began with G.)

PLAYER: "Was he a great novelist?"

LEADER: "No, it is not Galsworthy."

PLAYER: "Was he a great English humorist?"
LEADER: "Yes. It is Gilbert!"

The game is then started all over again with some other leader and some other initial. And questioner who, in being challenged, fails to give a correct name loses his right to all further questions, and the leading question need not be answered. The winner is the one who can keep the players at bay the longest.

YOU SAY IT WITH TWO LETTERS

Every player has pencil and paper; read out the following list of definitions and ask everyone to express the words which these definitions define, in two letters: For example, if you say "not difficult," they write the two letters, EZ. If you say "the number following 79," they write down AT. The following is a list of ten words which may be used. You can make up your own if you wish, and figures may also be used:

1. devoid of, barren (MT)
2. disintegrate (DK)
3. a girl's name (KT)
4. of whatever quantity (NE)
5. prior to (B4)
6. a girl friend (QT)
7. a fabric (PK)
8. an electrical unit (OM)
9. a metal (IN)
10. to lead in a particular field (XL)

Scoring, of course, is on a percentage basis, 10% for each correct answer.

WORD ASSOCIATION

This is a real psychoanalytical game, and one which is the best of all psychoanalysis. Word associations do give an insight into what you are thinking about, and what your complexes are. Tell your guests that you are going to give them one word and they must immediately write down on their papers a list of the first 15 words that pop into their heads. They must play fair and, in fact, they will have to play fair if you make the time limit extremely small. If you say "Barn," and count to 20 while they are writing as quickly as they can a list of 15 words, they won't have much chance to fake.

After they have all written the first 15 words that pop into their heads, have them write their names on their papers and exchange them with their neighbors. Now have each list read out and it is up to the guests to do the psychoanalyzing. You have no idea what outlandish words and peculiar associations will result!

HIGHBROW GAME

10 Games in One

Prepare a list of names of great authors, great composers or great artists of the past. Write each name on a separate piece of paper, fold it and toss it into a hat. When the guests arrive, have each one pick out a paper, open it, read the name written on it and immediately give some work done by that particular person. For example: Elsie Smith picks the name "George Eliot." She must immediately say, "George Eliot, Silas Marner" —(or some other novel of Eliot). John Jones picks the name "Beethoven." He must immediately say, "Beethoven, Moonlight Sonata"—(or some other work of Beethoven).

This game can be played with any number of variations. Instead of famous authors or composers or artists, familiar quotations could be substituted, and the person who picks the quotation must read it and give the name of its author. Instead of quotations, unfamiliar words could be used, and the guests would either have to define them or tell in what sense they are used. The game could also be done for presidents of the United States, kings of England, or states. A player who picks a presi-

dent would have to give the name of the president who preceded him. For example: If he picks Johnson, he must read—
"Johnson, Kennedy." If he picks George V, he must read—
"George V, Edward VII." In the case of states, he must give
the capital, thus: "Texas, Austin."

ALIBI

This game is particularly entertaining and amusing if there
are some lawyers among your friends.

A man and a girl are told that they will be accused of a murder which was committed at such-and-such a place and time.
They are then sent out of the room and given ten minutes to
build up the strongest alibi that they can to prove their inno-
cence. They are told before they are sent out that each one
will be examined separately and their alibi must stand up
against this examination.

While the "accused" are out, a prosecuting attorney is selected, as well as a stenographer. The rest of the players are the
jury. The prosecuting attorney may ask any questions he likes
in order to break down the alibis of the defendants. Here is a
typical procedure:

Let us say that the murder was committed May 15th in New
York between 9 and 10 P.M. The girl is brought in.
P.A.: "Where were you between 9 and 10 P.M. on May 15th?"
GIRL: "I was in Newark visiting a sick cousin."
P.A.: "What train did you take?"
GIRL: "The 8:25 P.M."
P.A.: "Did anyone go with you?"
GIRL: "Yes, my friend Harry."
P.A.: "What train did you take back?"
GIRL: "The 11:46."
P.A.: "Did Harry return with you?"
GIRL: "Yes."
P.A.: "What did you do on the train going out?"
GIRL: "We talked about my sick cousin."

P.A.: "Where does your sick cousin live?"

GIRL: "36 Market Street, Newark."

P.A.: "Did you take a taxi or a bus from the station to your sick cousin's?"

GIRL: "A taxi."

P.A.: "That's all. Now bring Harry in."

Harry enters and is asked practically the same questions. If he and the girl have built up a strong enough alibi, he will be able to answer all the questions the way the girl did, but if they haven't covered all the possible points that might come up, there will surely be a contradiction. Maybe Harry will say a sick *aunt* instead of a sick cousin. Maybe he will blunder on the train times or the bus instead of the taxi from the station. There are many things that will break a weak alibi and it is up to these players to match their wits against the Prosecuting Attorney. Naturally the perfect alibi wins the game and the "lookers-on" are the judge and jury.

INITIALS

Before the guests arrive prepare a list of well-known people and have as many copies of this list as there are guests. When you are ready to play this game, hand each guest a list and tell them all that they are to write after each name two or three words (as the case may be) which will be most appropriate to the name and, at the same time, begin with the initials of that name. Here are several examples:

1. Albert Einstein—Amazingly Erudite
2. Lyndon B. Johnson—Let's Be Just
3. Ed Sullivan—Every Sunday
4. Frank Sinatra—Fabulous Singer

The game can also be done with the names of the guests present if they all know one another well enough.

When everyone has finished, ask each guest in turn what he had for No. 1 and take a vote on the best answer. Do the same for No. 2 and take a vote on that. Do the same for No. 3 etc. The winner will be the one who gets the greatest number of votes. Of course the list may be as long or as short as you wish.

WHAT'S WRONG?

Let your guests make a thorough survey of the room. Allow five minutes for this and then send them all into another room while you make a number of alterations in the first room. Be sure that you write down these alterations so there can be no mistake. Now call your guests back, hand them each a pencil and paper and ask them to write all the changes that have taken place. Allow five minutes for this. The person with the greatest number of correct answers wins.

THE TRIP

This game is played in a crowd. Let two other people in on the secret and keep the rest of the crowd guessing. The secret is that the articles taken on the trip must begin with the same initials as the name of the person who says he is going to take them. For instance, John Smith might say he is going to take a Jersey and a Sweater. Oscar Carhard might take Old Clothes, etc. If two or three people know the secret of this game, it will be all the more fun.

Here is the way a typical "Trip" game would be played: The host (who knows the secret) starts in by saying, "I am going on a trip next week and expect to take with me some Eels, Mice and Shoes. What are you going to take?" Of course we are assuming that the host's initials are E.M.S. The next player, not being in on the secret, will mention articles which do not coincide with his initials and will be told that he cannot take those—he must choose something else. Of course he won't choose things that will coincide with his initials unless it is by sheer accident. After telling him repeatedly that he cannot take the articles he names, the next player (who is in on the secret) is asked what he or she is going to take. The response will be correct. If the name is Stanley Swain, he might say a Saucepan and Scissors and the host, of course, will allow him to take them.

After this questioning has gone the rounds, it will be interesting to see who is the first to catch on to the code—that player will win the game.

QUOTATIONS

Arrange your guests in a semicircle and, starting at one end, ask that person to complete the quotation which you are about to start. If he completes it correctly he remains in the game and if he doesn't he is out. Now give the next person another quotation to complete and so on until, by the process of elimination, only one person is left. He or she will be the literary light and winner.

Of course it would be best to write down a number of familiar quotations before the guests arrive so that you will have them handy for the game. Always stop them abruptly about at the middle so that the player will have a better chance of answering it. Here are some suggestions:

YOU   PLAYER
"The curfew tolls the knell" . . . . . . "of parting day."
"Friends, Romans, Countrymen" . . . "lend me your ears!"
"Give me liberty or" . . . . "give me death."

You can collect hundreds of familiar quotations from the Bible or Shakespeare or famous people in politics.

EARTH, AIR, FIRE, WATER

Arrange everyone in a circle. Start off by saying one of the above words and either pointing to or touching any guest at all. Suppose you say "Air" and touch John Jones. He must immediately respond by naming something that lives or travels in the air. He may say "bird" or "airplane," but he has to say it before you count ten with moderate speed. If he does, you continue. You may say "Water" and point to or touch some other guest. His answer must be prompt and correct. He may say "fish," "boat," or anything that lives in or travels on water.

There must be no response to the word "Fire." If you say "Fire" and point or touch someone, he must not answer. If he does, he is out. There must be no repetition in this game and if you should say "Air" again and touch somebody else, he cannot say "bird" or "airplane." He must say "sparrow" or "zeppelin." If he repeats anything that has been said before, he is out. The last player to remain, of course, is the winner.

PROPER NAMES

This game is a variation of I AM THINKING OF A NAME. One of the guests leaves the room while the rest agree on a proper name (the name of a person or place). When he is called back he must ask each person in turn a question in an effort to find out what name was chosen. So far this is just like 20 questions. The difference, however, is in the answers. Unless the name is actually guessed each answer must be in the form:

"No, it is not . . . . Yes, but it's not . . . ."

The missing word in the above must begin with the same letter as the name chosen and the answer must be true.

Suppose Beethoven were chosen as the proper name. The questioning might go something like this:

Q. Is it a city in England?
A. No, it is not *B*irmingham.
Q. Is it a man?
A. Yes, but it's not *B*unyon.
Q. Is he alive?
A. No, it is not *B*yron.

Q. Is he a musician?
A. Yes, but it's not *B*ach, etc.

Anyone failing to answer correctly is declared out. The winner is, of course, the last one out.

ONE MINUTE TO GO

This is one of the most fascinating games we know. You, as the host or hostess, hold a watch in your hand and tell your guests that you are going to name a letter (not "X"). After you name the letter, the person on your right must name as many words as he can, beginning with that letter, within a minute. It is up to you to be the time keeper and scorer.

Suppose you name "H." As soon as you are ready to start, say "GO!" and the person on your right will start pouring out words beginning with "H," like "hat," "heaven," "hold," "hemp," etc. You must keep track of the words and, at the end of a minute, stop him. If he gets more than 23 words, he is doing very well. When this is finished some other letter is called for and the same thing takes place. The one who gets the most words, of course, wins the game.

FORBIDDEN LETTER

Everyone must agree to omit a letter when he answers the questioner, but the questioner need not bother to omit it. The questioner may ask any question he likes, and the person answering it must be sure to use words that do not contain the forbidden letter. Suppose you have all agreed to omit the letter "I" from the answers. The questioner may say to one of the guests, "How do you like this game?" The player cannot reply, "I like it" or "I do not like it," because these words contain the letter I. His answer could be, "Pretty well." If he answers wrongly he is out. Each player in turn answers a question, *always omitting the forbidden letter in his answer*. After once around a new letter may be chosen.

DEFINITIONS

Make a list of words that are difficult to define and spring them, one at a time, on your friends, asking for the shortest and most accurate definition. Of course the dictionary will be your authority. It is better to take abstract or difficult words than simple ones.

Here is a list which will be suitable to start with:

1.	time	6.	color
2.	honesty	7.	music
3.	shadow	8.	sylph
4.	passion	9.	matter
5.	radiation	10.	fluency

EXPRESSIONS

This is an old game, but it never fails at a party. Select someone who thinks he or she can register various emotions and let him face the audience and "go to it." If you want to help him along, give him a list of expressions, each one numbered, and let him first say the number and then register the expression. It is up to the guests to figure out what expressions are registered.

Here is a list which ought to be helpful: anger, rapture, fear, disappointment, awe, surprise, excitement, scorn, remorse, anxiety, superiority, inferiority.

I SENTENCE YOU

This is an excellent little game to play in small groups. It is required that everyone make a sentence from the letters in a given word—any word—in a given time. Suppose we say the time limit is 30 seconds and we take the word "chair." The person called upon must respond with a five word sentence, the initial letter of each word being the letters of the word "chair," thus—"Clarence has an idiotic relative." The more humorous the sentences the better, and it is up to you to set the time limit—if you find 30 seconds to short, allow 45 seconds, or a minute. Change the word each time, but don't let it get larger than five or six letters.

THERE'S SOMETHING WRONG

It is a simple matter to provide your guests with fun by making up a number of sentences and putting them, without any punctuation at all, in a paragraph to be read aloud by one guest in front of the others. The sentences should not commence with ordinary words, but preferably with words like "being," "after," "under," etc., which help to connect the previous sentence in the most ridiculous manner. The following nonsense is a combination of fifteen sentences and is typical. Let someone read this aloud and see what effect it has on the rest of the people present. It case anyone claims that it makes no sense at all, it may easily be divided into its fifteen sentences and punctuated as shown.

I am sorry said the Duke but I can't eat any beautiful young girls what a delightful sight to see after one's leg has been in a cast all week it is wise to be careful about the eyes is the best place for specs unless they come early they go home with a shriek and a yell they admitted they forgot which side of a postage stamp to lick should not be difficult to find out because of a fire in the midtown section all schools were closed and it will require complete refilling of all bottles only if and when it is not damaged will they consider it is it correct to say none is here we are again for the last time I ask you why under no circumstances should they go out to be or not to be that is the question.

1. "I am sorry," said the Duke, "but I can't eat any."
2. Beautiful young girls—what a delightful sight to see!

3. After one's leg has been in a cast all week, it is wise to be careful.
4. About the eyes is the best place for specs.
5. Unless they come early they go home.
6. With a shriek and a yell they admitted they forgot.
7. Which side of a postage stamp to lick is not difficult to find out.
8. Because of a fire in a midtown section, all schools were closed.
9. And it will require complete refilling of all bottles.
10. Only if and when it is not damaged will they consider it.
11. Is it correct to say "none is"?
12. Here we are again!
13. For the last time I ask you, "Why?"
14. Under no circumstances should they go out.
15. To be or not to be, that is the question.

MEMORY GAME

This is a lot of fun in a group of people. It requires practically no preparation. Make a list of ten or fifteen words—any words that come into your head. Number each word and read the list slowly to your guests. You might even read it twice, to make the game a little easier. After you have finished, ask each guest in turn what the word corresponding to a given number on your list is.

For example, here is a list of ten words:

1.	baby	6.	egg
2.	lamp	7.	soup
3.	typewriter	8.	book
4.	orange	9.	overcoat
5.	letter	10.	cloud

Now read this list to your guests as follows: "Number 8 is book, number 2 is lamp, number 5 is letter" etc. Read them in any order you wish except the right order. When you have finished the list select one particular guest and ask him to repeat the entire list in the correct numerical order. It is by no means easy to do and the first one to do it correctly wins the game. Of course the list may be extended to as many words as you wish and the more disassociated the words are, the better it will be.

ADVICE

Each girl is supposed to whisper a piece of advice to a boy who writes it down. Each boy then whispers a piece of advice to a girl and she writes it down. The papers are marked "B" or "G," determining whether they are meant for a boy or a girl, and are collected. After they have been collected, they are put in a hat and redistributed, the boys taking the "G's" and the girls taking the "B's." Each one in turn reads what is on his slip.

THE B GAME

This is an excellent game for small groups. Arrange the players in a circle and read the following list of things to do. Each player is allowed ten seconds to think of the right answer. If he fails, he is out of the game and the player next to him must answer for him. The game has to do with adding the letter B to a word (the definition of which you are to mention), to get another word (the definition of which you are to mention). Here is an example: put B in front of a garden tool and get a device that stops automobiles and trains. The answer is RAKE—BRAKE. Here is another: put B in front of the organ of hearing and get an animal. The answer is EAR—BEAR.

Read the following list to your players and be sure to get the right answer to one of them, in the given time, before you go to the next one.

PUT B BEFORE:

1. an animal and get a container (ox—box)
2. a small portion of hair and get a chunk of wood (lock—block)

3. a dirty insect and get a shirtwaist (louse—blouse)
4. a rowing implement and get an animal (oar—boar)
5. aged and get brazen (old—bold)
6. a crest of a hill and get a card game (ridge—bridge)
7. a rodent and get a spoiled child (rat—brat)
8. a grain and get a water craft (oat—boat)
9. the finish and get a sharp change of direction (end—bend)
10. a weight and get what a rubber ball does (ounce—bounce)
11. a deficiency and get the absence of color (lack—black)
12. a weaving machine and get what flowers do (loom—bloom)
13. morally obligated and get purchased (ought—bought)
14. to appear to be lame and get an airship (limp—blimp)
15. part of a track and get a nautical term for rope (rail—brail)
16. to devour and get overcome (eat—beat)
17. a preposition and get a boxing match (out—bout)
18. to hurry and get to sweep or rub (rush—brush)
19. a connecting word and get a number of musicians (and—band)
20. to disembark and get mild and soothing (land—bland)
21. the final one and get an exposion (last—blast)
22. a sudden attack and get something tied with ribbons (raid—braid)
23. what most of us can do and get what most of us eat (read—bread)
24. correct and get brilliant (right—bright)
25. a chess man and get a stream of water (rook—brook)

THE M GAME

This game is a variation of THE B GAME; here, M is the key letter. The rules are the same.

PUT M BEFORE:

1. qualified and get a girl's name (able—Mable)
2. a high card and get a medieval weapon (ace—mace)

3. a beverage and get something of interest to a young girl (ale—male)
4. to a man's name and get a marred woman (Adam—madam)
5. the plural form of "to be" and get a female horse (are—mare)
6. a craft and get a selling center (art—mart)
7. "to point" and get "to wound" (aim—maim)
8. a quantity and get much (any—many)
9. a curved overhead opening and get uniform walking (arch—march)
10. assistance and get a young girl (aid—maid)
11. a biblical water craft and get a visible sign (ark—mark)
12. the past tense of eat and get your spouse (ate—mate)
13. sick and get a busy place (ill—mill)
14. aged and get a form (old—mold)
15. solid water and get rodents (ice—mice)
16. anger and get mud (ire—mire)
17. an ancient poem and get a manner (ode—mode)
18. employment and get a poet's inspiration (use—muse)
19. a writing fluid and get a valuable fur (ink—mink)
20. consume and get a food (eat—meat)

KEEP THEM GUESSING

The object of the following game is to keep the players guessing until someone discovers the hidden formula.

The hidden formula is always given in the first sentence but only the sharpest player will notice it. Players may ask as many questions as they like and you must always answer according to the rule. It is up to the players to discover this rule. Here are three games; play only one in an evening.

Read the following and then answer all questions:

1. My uncle has eyes but can't see everything. He can see a nickel but not a dollar. He can see a girl but not a boy. He can't see men and women but can see children. He can't

see buses or motorcycles but can see taxis . . . (Answer all questions.)

(The formula here is that your uncle can see anything with the letter *i* in it and can't see anything that does not have the letter *i* in it. This clue was given when you said he had eyes. If a player asks if he can see a newspaper, the answer, of course, is, "No, but he can see magazines." Can he see a boat? "No, but he can see an engine," etc.)

2. My aunt likes tea but not coffee. She doesn't like fish but does like fruit and vegetables. She eats potatoes but not corn or beans. She likes the city but not the suburbs, etc . . . (Answer all questions.)

(The formula here is that your aunt likes anything with the letter *t* in it and doesn't like anything that does not have the letter *t*. This clue was given when you said she liked tea.)

3. My twin brother and I like tennis and baseball but not golf. We both love swimming but don't like skating. We like apples and jelly but don't like plums and jam. We like to paddle but don't like to row, etc . . . (Answer all questions.)

(The formula here is that you both like anything that has a double letter in it . . . te*nn*is, baseba*ll*, swi*mm*ing, etc. and don't like anything without double letters. The clue was given when you said your twin brother and you.)

PROVERBS

This is one of the oldest and still one of the best games ever devised. One person is sent out of the room while the remaining people agree on a proverb. The absent player is then called back and is told to ask each player a question—any question at all. The answer to each question asked will contain one word of the chosen proverb in the order that it appears in that proverb. It is up to the questioner to guess the proverb from the answers he receives.

Here is a typical game:

Suppose the proverb is *You can't have your cake and eat it too*. The answer to the first question must contain the word *you*. The answer to the second question must contain the word *can't*.

The answer to the third question must contain the word *have*. The answer to the fourth question must contain the word *your*, and so on.

QUESTIONER: "How do you feel today?"

1ST PLAYER: "*You* ought to know."

QUESTIONER: "Would you like to come over next Friday evening?"

2ND PLAYER: "I'd like to but I *can't*."

QUESTIONER: "Have you read any good books lately?"

3RD PLAYER: "I *have* no time for reading."

QUESTIONER: "Have you any brothers?"

4TH PLAYER: "Yes I have one a little older than *your* brother."

QUESTIONER: "Are you enjoying this party?"

5TH PLAYER: "Certainly, especially if they have ice cream and *cake*."

Up to this point there have been no telltale words to give the proverb away. The word *cake* is the first clue but it may go unnoticed by the questioner who continues:

QUESTIONER: "What are you doing to-morrow?"

6TH PLAYER: "Bill *and* I expect to go over to see mother."

QUESTIONER (*completely baffled*): "What do you like to do most?"

7TH PLAYER: "I like to *eat*."

Now the questioner gets suspicious. He has heard the word *cake* and now he hears the word *eat*. *Eat* must be the clue word in the last answer because no other word is of any importance. After a little thought he might say: "You can't have your cake and eat it too," and the game is over and a new proverb chosen.

In selecting proverbs (or advertising slogans, for that matter) be sure to select ones that are not too obvious. In "A stitch in time save nine," the word "stitch" may not fit into an answer properly and the proverb is guessed before it is started. Be sure not to lay any stress or emphasis on the key words or else you will give the whole thing away. If you select an advertising slogan or a familiar quotation be sure to tell the questioner before he starts.

YOU WILL NOT LAUGH OR SMILE

This is an unusually funny game to be played in small and medium sized groups. The object of this game is to make a selected person laugh or smile against his will.

One person is selected to come up with a timekeeper, face the crowd and answer as many foolish questions with equally foolish answers as possible in a minute. If he laughs or smiles during this minute, he is out of the game. If, on the other hand, he succeeds in keeping a perfectly serious expression (which will be very difficult), he is the winner (provided nobody else who is selected keeps perfectly serious). Of course the rest of the people may laugh or smile as much and as often as they want—the more they laugh the better, because laughter is contagious and will weaken the seriousness of the selected player who must keep on being serious for a whole minute.

Before the guests arrive, think up a number of foolish questions and write each one on a separate piece of paper. These are to be distributed and read by the players in case they can't think up foolish questions for themselves. They don't have to use your questions if they don't want to—they are there just in case foolish questions don't come fast enough. Make up silly questions that best fit the people you are having, but don't get personal or don't ask things that may embarrass anyone.

Here is a typical game:

Dorothy is selected to start the game off. She faces the people and tries to keep a perfectly serious expression. When the timekeeper says "go!" we get something like this:

A PLAYER (*dramatically*): "What would you do if, on a dark night, you saw two husky clothespins hold up a pair of pants?"

DOROTHY (*seriously*): "I'd try to see who was in the pants."
   (*Everyone laughs but Dorothy who keeps a serious expression.*)

A PLAYER: "Suppose your husband were a lawyer, and the case he was trying fell on him. What would you do?"

DOROTHY (*smiling at her wit*): "I'd assume that the case was appealing enough to be appealed."
   Dorothy is out of the game because she smiled. Fred is now chosen and he must stand up and take it for a whole minute, just the way Dorothy tried to do.

ALPHABET PAIRS

This game is highly entertaining for any size group. Like GHOSTS IN MODERN DRESS, this game has to do with pairs of words which are commonly associated with each other. Instead of stringing them along as we did before, we will tie them to the alphabet. Name any letter and let each player in turn mention two commonly associated words, the first word to begin with the letter of the alphabet in the order that it comes to him and the last word to begin with the letter named. If *B* is the letter named, the first player should mention two commonly associated words, the first word to begin with *A* and the second *B,* the next player's two words will begin with *B* and *B,* the next player's two words with *C* and *B,* the next player's with *D* and *B* and so on down through the alphabet.

Here is a typical game:

YOU: "The letter I choose is *B*."
1ST PLAYER: "At Bat."
2ND PLAYER: "Better Business."
3RD PLAYER: "Candy Box."
4TH PLAYER: "Dead Broke."
5TH PLAYER: "Empty Barrel."

6TH PLAYER: "Flea Bite."
7TH PLAYER: "Good Bye."
8TH PLAYER: "House Broken."
9TH PLAYER: "In Bad."
10TH PLAYER: "Jealous Blonde."
11TH PLAYER: "Knitting Box."
12TH PLAYER: "Lazy Bones."
13TH PLAYER: "Money Back."
14TH PLAYER: "New Broom."

etc.

If any player hesitates too long at his turn or can't supply the two words, he is out of the game. Omit the letters *X* and *Z*.

THE SECRET FORMULA

This is another hilarious game which is particularly amusing to either large or small groups but not quite so amusing to the one who is selected to do the guessing. It should be played by people who know each other fairly well because the questions asked will be of a somewhat personal nature and the answers, while apparently false, are all absolutely true.

Select some good-natured guest to do the questioning and tell him to leave the room while you explain a certain formula to the rest of the people. While he is away tell each person in the room that he is to answer all questions *truthfully,* the way the *person sitting at his left* would answer them. If, for example, Miss Jackson is sitting to the left of Mr. White, Mr. White must answer any question asked of him truthfully from the standpoint of Miss Jackson.

He would answer a question like: "What kind of pipe is that you are smoking?" with: "I'm not smoking a pipe—I never smoked a pipe in my life!" Since he is obviously smoking a pipe, this sounds like a lie to the poor questioner but it is a lot of fun to the others. Miss Jackson, of course, answers for the person on her left (who should be a man). The guests should be arranged so that two men are next to each other in one part of the room and two girls are next to each other in the opposite part of the room. All the others should sit evenly mixed—a man, a girl, a man, a girl, etc.

Now call in the poor, unsuspecting and good-natured questioner and tell him to ask each player a more or less personal question, which will be answered truthfully according to a certain formula which he must discover. Only one question to a person is allowed.

Here is a typical game:

QUESTIONER (*to Mary who is sitting to the right of Harold, to whom she is engaged*): "Mary, when are you going to marry Harold?"

MARY: "I marry Harold?—Never! What do you think I am?"
(*This, of course, perplexes the questioner and causes much laughter among the players.*)

QUESTIONER (*to Harold who is at the right of Jane*): "That's a nice tie you have on, where did you get it?"

HAROLD: "I have no tie on—I never wear ties!"
(*More amazement from the questioner and more laughter from the crowd.*)

QUESTIONER (*to Jane who is sitting to the right of Mary—Jane is Fred's wife*): "What did you and Fred have for breakfast this morning, Jane?"

JANE: "I had grapefruit but I don't know what Fred had because I never had breakfast with him—that is I *hope* I didn't!"
(*By this time the questioner is completely baffled and the players are in stitches.*)

The questioner keeps going around the group asking questions of each one and getting what seem to him to be completely crazy answers. He should always ask questions of a somewhat personal nature—preferably having to do with visible things like clothing, make-up, etc. This will give him enough help to find the mysterious formula—but he won't find it before your guests have exhausted themselves with laughter!

INTELLIGENT READING

Call for a volunteer to come up and read this. If he fails call another. The first person who succeeds in reading the following two paragraphs intelligently, *without laughing or smiling*, wins this game. The reader must not only read it but he must explain it—and keep a straight face while everyone else laughs. Here are the two unpunctuated pieces of foolishness:

1. HAVE & HADD COMPANY

Mr. I. Have went into business with Mr. U. Hadd to form the firm of Have & Hadd. The following year the partnership broke up because:

While Have had to have Hadd Hadd did not have to have Have had Hadd had to have Have Have might not have had to have Hadd after Hadd had had Have and Have had had Hadd Hadd knew he didn't have to have Have while Have knew he had to have Hadd of course Hadd had half of what Have had and Have had half of what Hadd had so Hadd had to give Have his half and then Have had the half Hadd had had the half Hadd had and the half Have has gave Have entire ownership in Have & Hadd.

2. HOW SHOTT SHOT KNOTT

This is the old story of Shott and Knott who fought a duel. The story, however, has a new plot which is:

While Shott was supposed to have shot Knott the shot that Shott shot which was supposed to have shot Knott really had not shot Knott we think that Knott was shot by Shott's shot but maybe not if Shott had not shot that shot that shot Knott Knott might have shot a shot at Shott if the shot that Shott shot that shot Knott had been shot by Knott and not Shott Shott would have been shot by Knott and Knott not shot by Shott it's rot that Shott's shot shot Knott even if Knott was shot and Shott was not if what Shott shot was not Knott then what shot shot Knott?

CODE GAMES

The two code games that follow are both fascinating and full of mystery. After doing one of them a few times to the amazement of your guests get them to try to tell you how it is done. In a few cases you will be safe in offering a prize to anyone who can correctly explain the code, because, simple as the code is when you know it, it is just as difficult to guess!

In these code games, you must have a confederate who knows the code as well as you do. You and your wife or husband can do it together. If you care to, you can select a confederate from the guests, take him quietly inside without anyone knowing it, and show him the code. Of course it is preferable to have one of the guests do it with you—it won't look quite so "fishy" to the other guests.

CODE GAME A

Send your confederate out of the room and let the guests choose any object in the room. Call in your confederate and, assuming a pose of deep concentration, point to various objects in the room *without saying a word!* When you finally point to the object selected your confederate will say, "That's it!"

This will completely mystify everyone in the room! After all, not a word or a look passed between you and your confederate. How on earth is it done?

It is so simple that it is laughable! You merely agree beforehand with your confederate on an object that you will point to immediately before the selected object—and that is all there is to it. The object pointed to just before the one in question can be any one of the following:

    a. Any object with legs such as a chair, table, piano, person, dog, etc.

b. Any object which is black or in which black predominates.

c. Any object made of wood or in which wood predominates.

d. Any object which is circular such as an ash tray, a round table, a half dollar, etc.

Remember to agree on *ONE* of these four. If you agree on *a* then be sure to point to a table or a chair *just before* you point to the object selected and be sure NOT to point to a chair, table or anything else that has legs until that time.

If you agree on *b* don't point to anything that is black until you are ready and then be sure that the next object you point to is the selected one. The same is true for *c* and *d*.

You will probably have to do this a number of times and it may happen that your guests will want to choose the objects to which you point. In this case say "they're directing me" to your confederate when he enters and *put your hand in your pocket* when pointing to the object selected.

CODE GAME B

This is the most astounding code of them all and because it is so mystifying it requires a little memory work on your part and the part of your confederate. Your confederate in this case should be either your husband or wife, or your brother or sister, or some other member of your family whom you see every day and with whom you can practice.

The code will enable you to tell the dates on coins, or the amount of money in people's pockets, or what colors are selected, while you are blindfolded in another room with the door partially shut.

The code was made up by Robert Heller, a famous magician. Don't attempt to change the code words. They have been tested and have proved to be the easiest. Learn them thoroughly before the party. Let your confederate do the same. Learn to send as well as to receive.

Here is the code. Memorize it thoroughly:

NUMBER	CODE WORD	COLOR
1	Say or Speak	Blue
2	Look or Let	Green
3	Can or Can't	Yellow
4	Do or Don't	Orange
5	Will or Won't	Red
6	What	Black
7	Please	White
8	Are	Grey
9	Now	Brown
0	Quick	Gold

In guessing the dates on coins it is only necessary to give the last two numbers. The first two digits will invariably be 19 so that you need to say only two sentences, the first word of each sentence being a code word.

Now, you go out of the room. Your confederate asks for a coin. Someone hands him a quarter dated 1913. All he need do is flash 13 to you which he does as follows:

"*Speak* up now. *Can* you tell the date?"

You hear *Speak* and *Can*, which means 1 and 3 and you holler back 19*13*.

Now someone else hands your confederate a half dollar dated 1924. He then says:

"*Look* out for this one. *Don't* be fooled by it!"

You hear *Look* and *Don't,* which means 2 and 4 and you holler back 1924.

Of course this code is good for guessing the amount of money in a guest's pocket. In this case the last two numbers are cents. If your confederate says "How much money has Harry?" and then says: "*Will* you tell me as quickly as you can? *Please* don't take so long. *Will* you let us have the answer?" you know that Harry must have $5.75!

Only one sentence is necessary for naming a chosen color. For example:

"*Can't* you guess?" is Yellow.

"*Look* carefully" is Green.

GAMES OF ACTION

HOW DO YOU FEEL?

This is a new kind of feeling game. It requires a little preparation beforehand, but it is certainly worth the trouble. Before the guests arrive, procure a number of paper bags—as many bags as there will be guests. Into each bag put pieces of the following:

1. A small chunk of bread
2. A small bit of soap
3. A small chip off a candle
4. A little piece of art gum (purchased at any art supply store)
5. A small chunk of modeling clay
6. A small piece of meat
7. A little wad of tissue paper (wet this just before you are ready to play the game)

and as many small pieces of odds and ends as you can think up. Be sure to have things which are difficult to distinguish. The piece of soap and piece of candle, the bit of art gum and piece of bread, for example, are similar feeling objects.

When you are ready to play this game, give each guest a bag full of these objects. Tell them that you are going to call for this or that and they are to take it out of the bag without looking at what they are doing. If you say "Bread," they are to put their hands in the bag, feel around for the piece of bread without looking into the bag, bring it out, and show it to everyone. Anyone who brings out the wrong piece must put it back in the bag again. The winner is the first one to have an empty bag. Of course, this game becomes easier as the bags get less full.

SOUP PLATE

This is more a hilarious stunt than a game, and it is sure to provide a great deal of laughter for everyone except the victim. Before your guests arrive have two soup plates half filled with water. Blacken the bottom of one soup plate by holding it over a lighted candle. After the guests arrive, call for a volunteer to play this game with you. Tell him that he must do *exactly as you do*. He must keep his eyes fixed upon you and when you smile he must smile, when you arch your eyebrows he must arch his eyebrows, etc. Give him the soup plate with the dirty bottom and keep the other soup plate in your hand. Have him stand up facing you, holding his soup plate in his left hand, just the way you do. Now tell him to watch every motion that you make and do the same, and bet him that he cannot do it. Tell him that not one man in one hundred has the observation to go through all the motions correctly.

Of course, the idea is to get him to smear his face up without knowing it, but this has to be done gradually. The first thing to do is smile—and he will smile; cough—and he will cough. Put your thumb into the water in the soup plate, take it out again and shake it—he will do the same. Put your right hand on your head for a second and take it down, and he will do the same thing. Do a number of other things and he will do the same each time. Now rub your index finger all around the bottom of your soup plate and then quickly move it across your foreead and both cheeks—he will do the same. But this time there will be considerable laughter, because his finger will be full of soot which will blacken his face without his knowing it. Of course, your face will not be blackened, since there is no soot on the bottom of *your* soup plate. If he doesn't catch on to the laughter of the crowd, you can do some other stunts and come back to this again, when he will dirty his face even more, much to the amusement of the rest.

Of course, the object of the water in the plate is so that he cannot turn it upside down. The object of having him watch you intently is so that he does not notice his dirtied finger.

Don't try this on anyone who is hypersensitive or who is not willing to be a good sport. Most people will take it good naturedly.

THE THREAD RACE

This is to be run by two teams, each composed of a man and a girl. It is to be run in two parts, man number 1 and girl number 2 (of opposing teams) run the first part. The man has a spool of white thread and the girl a spool of black thread. The man must tie the loose end of the thread to some object like a chair leg or a door knob. The girl must do the same thing. Now they must agree on a course of travel and, having agreed, they are to go as quickly as possible over this course with their spools of thread, winding (but not knotting) the thread around each object in their path. Suppose they go from the living room through the hall into the dining room, and back again to the living room where they started. As they run, they must pay out their thread, twisting it not more than once around each object they meet, but never knotting it. The number of obstacles must be the same in both cases—if the man twists his thread around five obstacles, the girl must twist her thread around some other five obstacles.

The first one back must immediately give his spool to his partner—man number 1, for example, gives his spool to girl number 1, and girl number 2 gives her spool to man number 2. This will give the man or the girl (as the case may be) a head start.

The object of the second part is to *wind up* the thread on the spool again. The second couple must, therefore, go over the same course carefully, winding the thread back on the spool and untwisting the thread from the obstacles without knotting or breaking it. The winner will obviously be the one who gets back to the starting point with the spool all rewound and intact. Knots are not allowed. Broken threads eliminate the racers.

When the first two teams have completed the course, the next two teams commence, and so on. The winners of each team may play one another to see who will be the final champion.

NEEDLE ARCHERY

Did you know that a needle with a short thread attached to it makes an excellent javelin? Try some out and see what weight needle and what length of thread goes best. Then make up your set of "javelins" by choosing as many colored threads as there are guests and distributing one or two to each guest.

Let each guest in turn throw his "javelin" at some particular mark on the rug or carpet. This target may either be a design in the rug, or it may be drawn on a soft blanket spread over a table, making rings with chalk on the blanket. It should be in the form of a bullseye, with concentric rings, and the guests stand far enough away to make throwing reasonable. You can work up a scoring system of your own, and award a prize to the person with the highest score. Of course, this may be repeated over and over again.

THE HAT GAME

This game is played with a man's hat and a pack of playing cards. The hat is turned upside down and placed on the floor of the room against one wall. Each player stands about ten feet away and tries to toss cards into the hat. If you think this is easy, just try it. Out of 52 cards it is doubtful if you can throw 15 into the hat. It is lots of fun, and, as far as we know, may require skill. This game lends itself to a number of different methods of scoring. For example, you can either go by the number of cards in the hat at a given distance, or you can go by the face value of the cards. If you throw in the ace of spades you might get ten points, where the two of clubs would only count one point. Make up your own system on this before you start to play.

THE KANGAROO

Lay out four rows of thin, light sticks. Place the sticks about three feet apart and have as many as the room will permit. Select a player for each row, and, at the word "GO," all players must start to hop on one foot over each stick until they arrive at the last stick. As soon as a player arrives at the last stick, he turns around, still on one foot, and starts back, only this time after he hops over each stick, he must stoop down and pick it up. If he drops a stick, he must immediately start all over again. If he loses his balance and stands on both feet he must also start over again. The winner will be the one who is the first to bring back all the sticks in his row.

SMILE

All the girls in the room are to face the men and try to make them smile or laugh. The girls may laugh, tell funny stories or do anything else they choose to get the men to "thaw out" and look cheerful. Naturally the men try hard not to laugh or smile and if any man is so "unmanly" as to give in and laugh or smile he immediately joins the girls and tries to get his fellow men to do the same. The surprise comes at the end of the game when only one or two men are left. These serious glum creatures think that they are going to win a prize or win the game while as a matter of fact they are each fined 10¢ for being the biggest killjoys at the party!

STORK'S NINEPINS

Select nine players to stand at one end of the room on one foot only. It makes no difference which foot and it doesn't matter if they change from one foot to the other every once in a while, but they must be on one foot all the time. Now choose three girls to be the bowlers and give each girl in turn a large ball (medicine or basket ball) and tell her to roll it between these human nine pins. As the ball nears them they will naturally feel quite uncomfortable and the chances are that some of them will either stand on both feet or lose their balance and fall over. In either case they will be disqualified. The one holding out the longest wins the game. Of course the girls take turns in rolling the ball.

NUMBER PLEASE

Choose sides and line up each side facing the other. Give each guest a number (which you may either pin on his coat or hang around his or her neck) and tell him that that is his official number. Side A has its numbers (from 1 to 9 including 0) and side B has the same. A judge is chosen to stand at one end of the room and pick numbers from a hat. Suppose he picks 365. He calls out "Side A—number 365." At this instant number 3, number 6 and number 5 rush out and form this number as quickly as possible. If they form 563, 635, 356 or any other combination but 365 they are sent back and side B is given a chance. This is done 10 times for each side and the side that gets the greatest number of correct numbers wins. In case you have more than ten on each side use duplicates, for example 1831, 6486, etc.

Of course the numbers that you put into the hat will have no duplicates unless the players have duplicates. The numbers in the hat should all be between 100 and 10,000 and should never have any two digits alike unless more than ten players on each side are playing.

OBSTACLE RACE

Select two people and tell them that they must walk, blindfolded, from one end of the room to the other without bumping into a number of obstacles which you will put in their way. These obstacles may be anything in the room such as chairs, stools, lamps, etc. Tell them to take a good look at the layout of the room before you blindfold them so that they will be able to know about where each obstacle is.

Now blindfold them and, while you are doing it have someone remove *all* obstacles in the room so that the two players will have clear sailing. Of course they don't know this and when they start out on the "race" they will proceed with unusual care and walk so foolishly through nothing at all that everyone will laugh. After a while remove the blindfold and let them see how foolish they were!

SO NEAR AND YET SO FAR!

Here is another amusing blindfold game. The idea is to walk across the room blindfolded while holding hands with another blindfolded person. It is anything but easy to do and looks so foolish when you get three couples doing it at the same time that it is sure to produce a great deal of laughter.

Blindfold three couples who must keep holding hands and not let go. At the word "GO" let them try to find their way to the goal at the other end of the room. They must not let go of one another or they will be disqualified. The couple reaching the goal first, of course, wins.

TUMBLE-TUSSLE

This is a parlor wrestling match played by two boys (two girls may play too if they are game) and is sure to bring plenty of laughs to the rest of the crowd!

Each boy is seated on the floor with his back to the other. His knees are bent up and his hands are clasped under his knees. While in this position his wrists are tied with a handkerchief and his feet are also tied with another handkerchief. Both boys are now quite helpless with their backs to one another. It is now up to one of them to knock the other over. To watch these two helpless boys try to "get one another down"

is really extremely funny. Of course the winner will be the one
who succeeds in knocking the other one over. This can be done
in pairs and the final winners fight it out for the championship.

SCISSORS GAME

Here is an old favorite which is always dependable. Arrange
your guests in a circle and give one of them a pair of scissors.
Tell him to pass the scissors to his neighbor saying the following:

"I receive this crossed and pass it uncrossed," as the case
may be.

Of course the scissors will be open or shut, depending upon
how each person passes it to his neighbor. Naturally everyone
thinks that if it is open it is crossed and if shut it is uncrossed.
If Mr. Jones receives it open and passes it shut he will naturally
say "I receive this crossed and pass it uncrossed" but that may
not be the case. It all depends on whether or not he has his *legs
crossed*—for the *legs* are the clue and not the scissors. Every-
time someone makes an error it is up to you to say "that is not
so" and correct him. When it comes to your turn you can
either cross your legs or uncross them and you will be saying
what is so, much to the amazement of the guests. You would be
surprised how few people will catch on to the clue. Keep it up
until someone discovers that it has nothing to do with the scissors but has to do entirely with the person's legs being crossed
or uncrossed.

BUBBLE RACE

This is a sort of basketball with a bubble. Two sides are
chosen and bubble pipes and soapy water provided for each
side. Each side must have a bubble blower, a fanner and a
goal man. The two fanners stand facing one another in the
center of the room. Each has a piece of cardboard or a fan

in his hand. At the word "GO" the bubble blower for side A blows a bubble and the two fanners try to fan this bubble over toward their respective goals. If the bubble bursts, the two fanners start over again at the point where the bubble has burst, the other bubble blower blowing the next bubble. The object is to get the bubble over the goal line.

SIMON SAYS

Divide your guests into two sides who sit opposite each other at a table. The object of this game is for one side to conceal a dime (which is moving among the players of one team) from the other side.

Start the game by tossing the coin to see which side shall have charge of the dime first. When this has been done a captain of the offensive team is selected and whatever he says goes. If any other member of the team gives a command and anyone on the opposing team obeys it, the coin is forfeited and the other side gets it.

Now suppose team A has the coin. The captain of team B says, as his first command "UP SIMON" whereupon everyone on team A puts his hands high in the air (fists closed of course, so that nobody will be able to see where the dime is).

The next command by captain B is "DOWN SIMON" whereupon all the players on team A place their hands under the table and may pass the dime from hand to hand if they wish. The next order is "ON THE TABLE SIMON" whereupon all hands must be slapped palms down on the table (be careful not to rattle the coin when you do this as it will give the whole thing away).

Captain B now has to locate the dime. He can either guess directly or work by the process of elimination. If he guesses directly and, pointing to one particular hand, says "it's under there!" he scores 5 points if he is right and the other side scores 5 points if he is wrong. Whichever side scores has the custody of the coin for the next time.

If captain B succeeds in eliminating all the players and finding the coin in the last player's hand then his side scores 5 points; if not, the opposing side scores 5 points. The game is 50 points.

One last word—remember that any member of the attacking team (team B in this case) may give a command to the other side but only the captain is to be obeyed.

RELAY RACES

This game is played with two highball glasses, two ice cubes and two bread boards. The players are lined up in two parallel rows, the same number in each row, to form two opposing teams.

Player No. 1 of each team starts with an ice cube in his glass and player No. 2 of each team holds the bread board flat on the palms of his hands, ready to "receive" the ice cube. At the word "GO" players No. 1 of each team pour their cubes onto the bread board held by players No. 2. The boards are then passed to the next players of each team as quickly as possible without "spilling" the ice cube and so on all the way down the line and back again to No. 1 where it is returned to the highball glass. The game is very much like "A NUTTY GAME," only it is played with ice cubes instead of walnuts.

BASEBALL

This game is sure to prove a winner with everyone who likes baseball. It is played with a marble on a bridge table and the properties are very simple. They are:

1 marble
2 strips of cardboard 2 inches wide and a foot long
3 cardboard bases about 1 inch square, pinned in their proper places at 1st, 2nd and 3rd base on the table

1 pencil and pad

As many teaspoons as there are players

There must be a pitcher, a batter and as many fielders as you choose, each fielder having a teaspoon. The more fielders there are the more they will get in one another's way and so help the opposing team. It is best to have four on each side; a pitcher, a batter and two fielders.

The pitcher starts by letting the marble roll down his cardboard chute toward the batter who must receive this marble and, without taking his cardboard chute off the table, roll the marble in any direction he chooses. As soon as the marble leaves the batter he must grab the pad and pencil and write FIRST BASE as fast as he can. In the meantime the fielders are catching the marble with their spoons (they must catch it as it leaves the table and not scoop it up off the table). The first thing that a fielder must do when he has caught the marble is to touch the batter out at first—or at the base to which he is "running." He does this by carrying the spoon with the marble in it over to the base and touching that base. He must do this before the batter writes his base. If he does, the batter is OUT; if he doesn't the batter is SAFE. There are no such things as strikes or balls or fouls.

The name of the NEXT base to which you are going is always written on the pad. If you happen to be on first and you try to go to second after your teammate has just rolled the ball, you must both write on the pad. You write SECOND BASE and he writes FIRST BASE.

I KNOW YOU

Blindfold half of your guests and arrange the chairs so that each blindfolded person will sit next to an empty chair. Now let the other half (those who are not blindfolded) sit in these vacant chairs so that each blindfolded person will sit next to one who is not blindfolded.

Now, starting with the first "couple," have the player who is not blindfolded sing a short song in a disguised voice. When he has finished it is up to his blindfolded neighbor to call him by name. If he does this correctly he may remove his blindfold, if not he must keep it on. In either case the next "couple" gets a chance and this keeps on until everyone has sung and guessed.

After each song and subsequent guess, the unblindfolded players get up and move around and exchange seats with one another. The last one to have his bandage removed gets the booby prize!

SPOONING CONTEST

This is a good game to play when the refreshments are served. Tie two teaspoons together with twine so that they are about 18 inches apart and pair off the guests so that a girl has one spoon and a boy has the other. At the word "GO" they are all to start eating the ice cream (which will not be so easy to do), and the first couple who finishes wins and is entitled to eat the next portion without any strings attached.

GET RID OF THE ORANGE

Arrange two circles, the girls on the inside and the boys on the outside. Give one of the boys an orange and one of the girls an ice cube and start things going. Both the orange and the ice cube are to be passed from one to the other—the orange going around the boy's circle and the ice going around the girl's circle. Now, as soon as you clap your hands or shout "STOP," the boy who happens to have the orange must buy the girl who happens to hold the ice cube a box of candy.

Of course the boys will try to get rid of the orange as quickly as they can while the girls will hold on to the ice cube as long as they are able (which will not be long). The boys must pass the orange in one direction while the girls pass the ice cube in the opposite direction.

FOLDING CHAIR RELAY RACE

This game is a whale of a lot of fun to do. Divide your guests into two teams with the same number of boys and girls on each team.

On the floor at one end of the room or hallway have two folded bridge chairs about four feet apart. The players are at the other end of the room and at the word "GO" the first couple of each team runs over to the chairs, the boys open them as quickly as they can and the girls sit down in them and count to ten rapidly. The girls then get up and the boys fold up the chairs as quickly as they can and leave them where they found them. These two couples then run back to the next two couples who are "rarin' to go" and the same thing takes place all over again. The team who finishes first wins the race.

PING PONG FOOTBALL

Divide the dining room table into four equal parts with the aid of a piece of chalk. Now pick two teams with a boy and a girl on each team and arrange them as shown in the diagram:

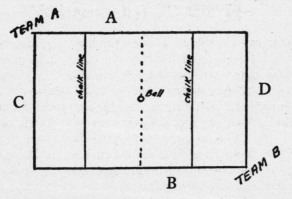

Each player now has his particular area to take care of and must act only when the ball comes inside that area. The ball (a ping-pong ball) is now placed in the center of the table and at the word "GO" players A and B start blowing the ball toward the opposite ends of the table, A's goal being one end and B's goal being the other end similar to a football field. As soon as the ball crosses the middle section into one of the end quarters it is up to player C or player D to blow it back again. The object of the game is to blow the ball off the table at one of the ends and make a "Blowdown." The team scoring the greatest number of "Blowdowns" in twenty minutes wins.

WHISTLE-CRACKER

Line up the guests in two parallel rows, the boys in one row and the girls in the other. Now give each guest a cracker which must not be eaten until the time comes. At the word "GO" the first boy and the first girl start to eat their crackers and as soon as they have finished they must whistle clearly, turn around and face the person behind who must immediately start to eat his cracker, finish it, whistle clearly, turn around and face the person behind him and so on all the way down the line. The first line to finish wins.

PAIRS TREASURE HUNT

This game requires a little preparation in advance. Before the guests arrive have a number of common articles numbered and hidden around the house. Each hidden article should have a small tag with a number tied to it. The number should be in two digits like 37 or 52 or 16. Now make out a list of articles that are commonly associated with the hidden articles. If you hid a comb, for example, you should have the word "brush" on the list. If you hid two eggs, you should have the word "ham" on the list, etc. Every article that is hidden must have a commonly associated on the list you prepare. Make as many copies of this list as there are guests, for each guest must have a list.

You now have a number of articles hidden and numbered.

You also have a number of lists—all the same—of companion
words to the hidden articles. When you are ready to play this
game, give each player a list and tell him to look for the article
that goes with the name. When he finds it he *must not disturb it*
but must write its number next to the correct word on his list.
The first player to get all the numbers completely and correctly, wins the game.

Here is a suggestion for a game:

LIST	ARTICLE TO HIDE	NUMBER ON ARTICLE
Ham	Two eggs	14 on one and 36 on the other
Cup	Saucer	51
Knife	Fork	21
Butter	Piece of bread	42
Comb	Brush	33
Lock	Key	27
Needle	Thread	16
Pen	Ink	30
Salt	Pepper	10
Pork	Can of beans	17

Now hide the ten objects mentioned in column two with
the numbers on them given in column three. The papers you
give to the players should look like this:

Ham and ....

Cup and ....

Knife and ....

Butter and ....

Comb and ....

Lock and ....

Needle and ....

Pen and ....

Salt and ....

Pork and ....

The first player turning in his paper with the correct numbers on the blank lines will be the winner. Obviously the num-

bers are there to prove that the player has found the object. After ham he should have 14 and 36, after cup he should have 51, after knife he should have 21, etc. All hidden articles must be left in place and not touched.

GOING AROUND IN CIRCLES

Arrange as many chairs in a circle as you have players and pin a large number on each chair so the players may see it but the occupants of the chair may not. These numbers may be from 1 to whatever number you have, or they may be various numbers like 63, 52, 16, 27, etc. As the game is confusing anyway, it would be best to start with numbers 1, 2, 3, etc. If you find this easy, then you can try it with the various numbers.

Each player knows his number when the game starts and must keep alert to his number as it changes.

The object of this game is to respond instantly when your number is called and to call another number different from the one that just called you. If you fail at this, everyone moves up one seat, you take the last seat and all the numbers change accordingly. It is when this happens that the game gets exciting. The player who goes completely around the circle of chairs, wins the game.

Here is how it works:

Player in chair 1 calls number 6. Number 6 must answer instantly and call some number other than number 1. Suppose he calls 4. Player number 4 responds instantly by calling any number other than number 6. If a player does not answer instantly or if a player answers when he shouldn't or if he calls back the number that just called him, everybody must get up and take the next chair. In this case, the player who was number 1 is now 2 and the player who was 2 is now 3, etc. This gets quite confusing after a while and if a number of changes have been made, it requires considerable concentration to keep from making errors. You can see that as soon as you get used to thinking of yourself as number 6 and you change to number 7, you are apt to be confused when numbers are called and are more apt to make errors.

The more errors, the more confusion will result, and the player who can keep moving from one chair to the next all the way round the circle of chairs without being obliged to take the last chair, because of an error, deserves a prize.

Since each chair has a large number pinned on it and since these numbers remain fixed as the players move around, it will be easy to identify the correct player. If number 5 answers and he is sitting in chair 6, it is an error and everyone must move again and take the number of the chair in which he sits.

LETTER BOXES

Before the guests arrive, place twelve small cardboard boxes in various parts of the house. Make them as inconspicuous as possible and label each box with the name of a state.

Now prepare about fifty or sixty small cards with the name of a city written on each; when you are ready to play this game call all the players together and give each player a card. When this is done, it is up to each player to write his or her name on the card and "post" it in the correct box. As nobody knows where these boxes are, it will not be so easy. As soon as a player finds the correct box and has "posted" his "letter" in it, he must return for another "letter" and hunt up another box to "post" it in. The person who gets the greatest number of "letters posted" wins the game.

Here is how it works:

Suppose you have named your boxes New York, Montana, California, Ohio, Maine, Pennsylvania, Missouri, Texas, Illinois, Massachusetts, Florida and Tennessee. These twelve boxes are placed inconspicuously in various parts of the house. Of course, the cities which you write down on the fifty or sixty small cards must be cities that are in these twelve states and they must be fairly large cities so there is no mistaking what state they go to. Your list might include such cities as New York, Chicago, Philadelphia, St. Louis, Cleveland, Boston,

Butte, Los Angeles or any other well known cities which may be found in any of the twelve states named above.

If ten people are playing, there should be five or six cities given to each player (one card at a time), but it may happen that Miss Brown is quicker than Mr. Watts and she is able to find the correct boxes faster. She finds the Montana box and "posts" her Butte "letter" in it and comes racing back to you for another city. Her next city might be Nashville and she finds Tennessee quickly and returns again for another city and so on. She might succeed in "posting" ten "letters" to Mr. Watts' two.

When all the cards have been given out, the boxes are collected and the "letters" counted. As each "letter" has the name of the person posting it written on it, it will not be difficult to see who has "posted" the greatest number of "letters" correctly and proclaim him the winner.

Of course, no player may tell another player where a box is after he has discovered it. All cities must be posted in their correct states, any city found in the wrong state box should be discarded.

DO THIS AND ADD SOMETHING

The players sit around in a large circle. One player starts the game by getting up, standing in the center of the circle and assuming a very foolish attitude. This done, he returns to where he was and the next player gets up, comes to the center of the circle, assumes the attitude of the previous player and adds an attitude of his own. This done, he returns to his place and the next player comes up, assumes the two previous attitudes and adds one of his own. As this keeps on going it gets funnier and funnier and you can imagine how ridiculous any man or girl will look going through ten or fifteen different motions like thumbing his nose, throwing his hands above his head, bending over and looking through his legs, jumping up in the air twice and hollering "Yippee!", stroking his sleeve, etc.

No player is allowed to add his motion until he has successfully imitated all the previous motions and attitudes in their correct order. If he fails to do this he is put out of the game. The game gets more and more difficult as it progresses and it won't be very long before most of the players have missed out and are disqualified. This will leave one or two players to go through all the antics and there certainly will be plenty to laugh at in watching it. The player to stay in the game the longest wins the game.

As an additional feature it should be added that no player may laugh or smile while going through his various motions and antics. The rest of the people may laugh as much as they want to but the performer must keep a straight face and do his stuff without any mistakes—otherwise he is out of the game.

NUT RACE

Divide the guests into two teams with the same number of players on each team. Have the teams face each other, standing about four feet apart. In front of each player, on the floor, place a walnut.

Now appoint two nut collectors to stand at the foot of each line with a basket or box while you stand at the head of the lines. At the word "GO" the first player of each team must pick up the walnut in front of him and hand it to the player next to him, who must pick up the walnut in front of him and hand both nuts to the third player, who must pick up the walnut in front of him and hand the three nuts to the fourth player, and so on. The last player, of course, has a handful of walnuts which he must give to the nut collector who puts them in the box and carries them back to the first player. The first player then takes all the nuts out of the box and the nut collector runs back to his original position, taking the empty box with him. As soon as he is back the first player starts passing one nut at a time to his neighbor who must pass it on until it gets to the empty box again. The first team to go through this and fill the empty box twice wins the game.

No player may bend over and touch the nut in front of him until he has received the nut from his neighbor. If he does he is disqualified. If a player drops a nut he must immediately pick it up. Of course nuts must be passed and picked up as fast as possible as this is a race between two competing teams.

A NUTTY GAME

Here is a less active version of NUT RACE.

Divide your guests into two groups and seat them in two rows of chairs facing each other. At both ends of each row, place a bowl. The first man in each row has a bowl beside him and in the bowl there are a dozen walnuts. At the word "GO" these two men begin "feeding" their respective sides with nuts. The nuts must pass from each player to his neighbor, one at a time, and as each nut reaches the other end of the line it is placed in an empty bowl. As soon as the 12th nut reaches the bowl at the other end of either line, the person at that end begins to return them in the same manner. The side which empties the first bowl and refills it again wins.

Nuts must be passed one at a time and must pass through each player's hands in turn. If a player drops a nut, he must pick it up before he passes the next nut to his neighbor. The nuts must go from a full bowl at one end of the line to an empty bowl at the other, and back again to the original bowl, in the shortest possible time. Another way to play this game is not to start the second nut going until the first nut reaches the empty bowl at the other end of the line. As soon as the last player drops this nut in the bowl, the first player starts the second nut going, etc.

BLIND SWAT

This is a real rough-house game, in which two boys take part. Give each one a rolled-up newspaper in the form of a club. Now blindfold both of them and tell them to hold hands (left hands only). They are not to let go under any circumstances.

While these two boys are thus blindfolded, they are to take the rolled-up newspapers in their right hands and hit one another with them. This will not be easy, since they are blindfolded and are holding hands—but it will be a lot of fun to watch. The score keeper will keep track of the number of hits scored in a set time limit, and, of course, the winner is proclaimed. You had better remove all breakable objects before starting.

RELAY RACE

Choose sides and have an equal number of couples on each side. This is a relay race, starting with two couples. It is best done in a long hall, starting at one end and racing to the other and back in the following unusual manner:

Two girls, assisted by two men, start to "race" from one end of the hall or long room to the other end and back again. The girls do the "racing" by stepping on paper or cardboard which the men put in front of them. At the word "GO" both men put down a piece of paper or card and both the girls immediately step on it. Both men then put down another piece of paper or card which both girls immediately step on. Both men then pick up the first piece of paper or cardboard and put it down again in front of the girls to be immediately stepped on, and so the race progresses, step by step, until one of the girls has traveled all the way to the far end of the hall or room and back again to start off a second couple. The paper or cards should be about 8 inches square and should be put as far in front of each girl as she can conveniently step. The girls are not allowed to jump or skip from one card to the next; they must step—and the "race" must progress by steps. The men must be extra quick in taking up the old piece and placing it in the new position. At no time is a girl allowed to step off the cards; if she does she is disqualified. As soon as one couple finishes, the next couple starts and so the race progresses until one side wins.

TISSUE PAPER RACE

While this is essentially a game for the youngsters, it is just as much fun for grown-ups—especially the dignified dowagers and elderly captains of industry who need to reduce.

At one end of the room or hall place two cushions on the floor. On each cushion put at least ten sheets of tissue paper, cut in squares about 1½" on each side. At the other end of the room have two empty glasses.

After choosing sides, start two players off (one from each side) by giving them each a teaspoon and telling them to run to the cushions, pick up one piece of tissue paper with the spoon, carry it on the spoon to the empty glass at the other end of the room or hall, and put it in the glass. The first one to do this starts the next player on his side going and so the race progresses until one side wins.

At no time must the hands or fingers touch the tissue paper and the teaspoon must be held horizontal all the time. If the paper falls off the spoon it must be picked up *with the spoon* and not with the fingers. It is not advisable to run with the spoon and paper because the wind thus created will blow the paper off the spoon and delay the player. This is a real case of the more haste the less speed and the wise player will walk carefully and slowly to the glass each time.

The first side to put all ten tissue papers in the glass wins the game.

PAPER STRIP TEASE

Prepare about twelve long strips of paper two inches wide and eight or ten feet long. You can get these from adding machine rolls or bolts of ribbon. Use only eight strips to start the game.

Now attach one end of each strip to a blank wall, about 42 inches above the floor and let the other end trail on the floor. The strips should be at least two feet apart so that eight players can work, one on each strip, while standing next to one another.

Each player is supplied with a scissors and instructed as follows:

"At the word 'GO' you must all start cutting your strip in half the long way without going off the strip. Each two players forms a team and the winner of each team will compete in the 'semi-finals.'

"Any player going off the strip is out of the game, and the first one in each team to reach the wall by cutting his or her strip lengthwise wins for his team.

"The contestants in the 'semi-finals' may use any of the cut strips. The strips they use will be only half as wide as they were and will have to be cut with twice as much care to prevent going off. The same rules apply to contestants in the 'semi-finals' as previously.

"The two winners of the 'semi-finals' will now race each other for the final honors and grand prize. This time each strip will be only a quarter as wide as it was originally and extreme care must be exercised. If a player goes off the strip, the other player wins."

The length and width of each strip is up to you. We suggest two inches wide and eight or ten feet long because this is most practical. You can make this game easier or more difficult by changing these dimensions.

The winner of this game certainly deserves a worth-while prize.

HUMAN HORSERACING

Select six players and pin a large number on the coat or dress of each player—numbers from 1 to 6 inclusive. These players are the human horses. Now stake out a course by placing markers on the floor at intervals of two feet. These will act as a guide for the "horses" who must not take any step longer than two feet. The course need not be a straight one; it can be across one room and through another and back again. It makes no difference just as long as you have guide markers to indicate the length of the two foot step.

Players that are not "horses" may bet on their particular "horse" and after the betting is all in the race starts. All six "horses" line up against one wall which is the starting line. A selected guest throws three dice and announces which players are to take a step forward. If he throws 2, 6, and 4, "horses" 2, 6, and 4 move one step forward. If he throws a double number that numbered "horse" takes two steps. If he throws a triple number, that numbered horse takes *six* steps forword. "Horses" are not allowed to move until the result of a throw of dice is announced. Of course the winner will be the "horse" who completes the course first. When the first race is over, six new "horses" may be chosen and the second race starts.

WHERE RIGHT IS WRONG

This game will test your guests' wits and ability to think quickly. The girls form a line and face the boys in another line. The lines are to be about three or four feet apart. You, as the host or hostess, stand at the head of both lines and ask questions which must be answered *truthfully* by the *boys* and *falsely* by the *girls*. If a girl answers a question truthfully, she is out of the game. If a boy answers a question falsely he is out of the game. All questions must be answered *immediately* and if anyone takes more than two seconds to answer he is out of the game.

Start the game by asking the first boy a question. *He must not answer* but the girl directly opposite him must answer *falsely for him*. Now ask that girl a question. *She must not answer* but the boy opposite her and next to the first boy must answer that question *truthfully for her*. This goes on until the end of the lines are reached and the questioning comes all the way back again to where it started. If anyone disobeys the rules he or she is disqualified and put out of the game. Here is the way a game might start.

YOU (*to first boy*): "How tall are you?" (Boy does not answer.)

GIRL (*opposite the boy*): 8 feet 7 inches.

YOU (*to first girl*): "How old are you?" (Girl does not answer.)

SECOND BOY: "About 22, as near as I can judge."

YOU (*to second boy*): "How much do you weigh?" (Boy does not answer.)

SECOND GIRL (*opposite boy*): "798 pounds."

YOU (*to second girl*): "What color hair have you?" (Girl is silent.)

THIRD BOY: "Brown."

This keeps up until someone makes a mistake—either answering out of turn or answering incorrectly according to rules. As each player makes an error he or she drops out of the game and it won't be long before there are only a few players left.

Be sure to ask questions that both the boys and the girls can answer. It is easy to lie but not easy to tell the truth because in most cases a boy doesn't know much about the girl opposite him. Ask the girls things which are visible so the boys can see what they are answering. Don't ask them anything personal or anything too abstract. The boy and girl who remain in this game the longest win.

PACK OF CARDS

Take as many cards from a pack as you expect players at the party and make up a story about these cards. You can describe a bridge hand in which these cards appear or you can write any other story you wish, but the names of the cards must be in the story. It is preferable to have your story written in advance and read it to the players when the time comes.

When you are ready to play the game you must have as

many chairs as there are guests while you must be standing. Now give each player a card and tell them all that you are going to read a story, and as soon as a particular card is mentioned the holder of that card must jump up, turn around once, and sit down again as quickly as he or she can do it. As you will be naming the cards right along in your story the players will be jumping up, turning around, and sitting down again in quick succession. Any player who fails to do this quickly and correctly is out of the game and his chair is taken away. When you come to the last card in your story say something about shuffling the pack, and as soon as the players hear this they all jump up and change places. This is your chance to get a seat, and it is up to you to take the first chair you can get. Someone will be left out because there is one less chair than there are players. He will be the one to read the story again, and the game starts all over.

Of course you can make up other stories. The original game was called "stagecoach" and a story was made up about a stagecoach and articles connected with it, such as horses, whip, driver, harness, shaft, etc. The game is played exactly as described previously, and when the narrator says, "Then the stagecoach turned over," everyone jumps up and changes seats.

There are any number of other stories that will fit this game, and you can choose any theme you like. Here are two suggestions:

BLOWOUT. Played as described. Players have names of auto parts, such as horn, engine, tires, wheels, etc. When "blowout" is mentioned everyone changes seats.

TRAIN WRECK. Played as described. Players have names of articles connected wtih a train, such as engine, coach, wheels, brakes, etc. When "wreck" is mentioned everyone changes seats.

PENCIL AND
PAPER GAMES

CONCENTRATION

Here is a chance to make everybody dizzy. As soon as you say "GO," tell your guests to do exactly as you instruct them and not to do anything you don't tell them to do. Then read the following paragraph slowly, but do not repeat it. Of course, each guest must be supplied with a pencil and paper, and the winner of the game will certainly be entitled to a great deal of credit even if there are no prizes offered. Here is what you read slowly to the guests:

Somewhere in the center of the paper write the word "hour." To the left of the word "hour," write "day."

If an "hour" is less than a "day," write "hour" under "day" unless there are more than five weeks in a month, in which case write "second" over "hour."

Now cross out "day" and write the number of months in a year to the left of the word "day" and the number of days in a week to the left of this.

If you have written "hour" under "day," cross out the "hour," which is to the right of "day" and write the number of weeks in a year over the word "day" unless there are as many days in a week as months in a year.

If there are as many weeks in a year as there are seconds in a minute, don't cross out the number of months in a year.

Now write the word "month" over the number of weeks in a year and cross out the number of days in a week unless there are more weeks in a month than days in a year.

If there are more days in a month than weeks in a year, do not underline the number of months in a year.

Cross out the word "month" only if a day has as many hours as two years has months.

The winner's piece of paper will look like this:

~~month~~
52

~~X~~ ~~12~~ ~~day~~ ~~hour~~
hour

SHIP GAME

Read the following to your guests and ask them to write the words represented.

1. What ship do you find in the country?   (township)
2. What ship is the most romantic?   (courtship)
3. What ship applies to your guests?   (friendship)
4. On what ship did Einstein travel?   (scholarship)
5. What ship belongs on the bench?   (judgeship)
6. What ship belongs in church?   (worship)
7. What ship is most hated in this country?   (dictatorship)
8. What ship is the best ship to educate?   (apprenticeship)
9. What ship is needed by certain political parties in the country?   (leadership)
10. What ship belongs to the English nobility? (lordship)
11. What ship belongs to the white collar man? (clerkship)
12. What ship is shared with somebody else?   (partnership)
13. What ship is bought and paid for?   (ownership)

BRINGING UP JUNIOR

Below you will find a list of professions and vocations for Junior. Read these to the guests and have them supply the name of the most appropriate food. For example: If you want your boy to be a plumber, give him leeks.

The correct answers are given in parenthesis after the vocation and these must not be read to the players. They are to write the most appropriate food for each of the following:

 1. shoemaker   (sole or eel)
 2. electrician   (currants)
 3. postman   (lettuce)
 4. lumberman   (chops)
 5. architect   (cottage pudding)
 6. gambler   (steaks)
 7. prizefighter   (punch or duck)
 8. subway guard   (squash or jam)
 9. diamond merchant (carrots)
10. geometry teacher   (pie)
11. flower expert   (cauliflower)
12. policeman   (beets)
13. sailor   (roe)

THE EGG GAME

Read the following list of questions to the players and ask them to supply the correct "eggs" name for each question. For example: No. 1. The eggs that set a pattern to follow should be: eggsample (example).

Of course, all answers begin with "ex" although for this game they are pronounced "eggs," like "eggspression" and "eggsistance." Here is the list:

1. Eggs that set a pattern to follow.   (example)
2. Eggs that almost drive me crazy.   (exasperate)
3. Eggs that are better than any others.   (excellence)
4. Eggs that are used for packing China.   (excelsior)
5. Eggs that give forgiveness.   (excuse)
6. Eggs that travel short distances.   (excursions)
7. Eggs that seal the doom of murderers.   (execution)

 8. Eggs that are always moving.   (exercise)
 9. Eggs that show themselves in public.   (exhibition)
10. Eggs that are in every theatre.   (exit)
11. Eggs that just are.   (exist)
12. Eggs that grow larger and larger.   (expand)
13. Eggs that try to make themselves clear. (explain)
14. Eggs that look into the future.   (expect)
15. Eggs that discover new lands.   (explore)
16. Eggs that are truly remarkable.   (extraordinary)

ABBREVIATIONS

Here is a list of common abbreviations which appear in our books and magazines and business correspondence all the time. How many of them can you identify?

What does each of the following mean?

 1. i. e.   (that is)
 2. viz.   (namely)
 3. e. g.   (for example)
 4. stet.   (let it stand)
 5. re.   (regarding—in reference to)
 6. etc.   (and so forth)
 7. ibid.   (ibidem—in the same place)
 8. inst.   (the present month)
 9. e. o. m.   (end of month)
10. do.   (ditto)
11. id.   (the same)

GAME OF NO MYTHSTAKES

Have the players identify what each of the following mythological characters represents:

1. Minerva   (wisdom)
2. Apollo   (sun)

3. Bacchus	(wine)
4. Diana	(moon)
5. Pluto	(underground)
6. Ceres	(season)
7. Mars	(war)
8. Mercury	(messenger)
9. Neptune	(ocean)
10. Vulcan	(blacksmith)
11. Venus	(beauty)
12. Atlas	(world)
13. Hercules	(strength)
14. Cupid	(love)

SHORTHAND GAME

Dictate to your guests the following story and have them write it down. At each blank space tell them to put 2, 3, or 4 dashes as the case may be. These dashes represent letters or numbers, the names of which form words. For example: If the story were about school life, you might say, *"He will — — in his studies."* The two blanks must represent the letters "X L" or the word "excel" to make sense. The first blank in the given story stands for "I V," meaning "ivy." Now go on from there.

Under the — — covered — — tree, sat her — — — —, the wife of the Governor of — — —. Although she was writing an — —, her thoughts were with her soldier boy who had been captured by the — — — the week — —. She was wondering just what terrible — — prison life would have on him. She knew that his — — nerve and unbounded — — — would keep him from doing — — thing drastic. She was nothing to — — for her life was decidedly — — without her boy! How she longed — — him and — — with him and she fervently prayed for the quick — — of the army and the end of the war.

ANSWERS

I V, L M, X L N C, I O A, S A, N M E, B 4, F X,
I N, N R G, N E, N V, M T, 2 C, 2 B, 6 S.

MISSING ADJECTIVES

This game never fails to raise the roof with laughter simply because it turns out to be so ridiculous.

The host or hostess must prepare in advance a good decription of the forthcoming party. This description should be about 250 to 300 words in length and should include the names of everyone at the party. Leave a blank space before each guest's name as shown in the sample letter.

The host or hostess now asks each guest in turn to name an adjective—the more outlandish, the better. As each adjective is named, the host or hostess writes it in the blank space provided, thus completing the story. Of course, your guests do not know what is going on—they have no idea that you are writing these adjectives before their names and it won't take much strength of the imagination to realize the effect of this ridiculous story when it is finally read to the company.

Of course, you can go a little further and leave out a few nouns. You could, for example, say: "a very informal . . . . . ," and call for both names and adjectives as the case may be. This will make the letter even more foolish. Try it! Here is a sample:

On Saturday evening at the home of . . . . . . Jane Doyle, a number of . . . . . . boys and . . . . . girls assembled for what they thought would be a . . . . . . time. The . . . . . . hostess played a number of . . . . . games which to the disgust of . . . . . Helen Heath, the . . . . . . Arnold Banks, the . . . . . . Oscar Noble, etc., etc.

A few of the . . . . . . people at this . . . . . . party seemed to enjoy these . . . . . . games. Among these were such . . . . . . people as the . . . . . . John Brown, etc., etc.

BIBLE GAME

This game will test your knowledge and your guests' knowledge of the Bible. Of course the one who gets the most names correct wins the game.

Following is a list of eleven biblical characters. The first letter of each name is the same as the last letter of the preceding name; for example, the answer to No. 1—A prophet who stood for justice—is Amos, the answer to No. 2 must be a character beginning with the letter "S." The answer to No. 3 must be a character beginning with last letter in No. 2, and so on. All the answers are names of biblical characters—single names. How quickly can you find them?

1. A prophet who stood for justice. (Amos)
2. Called Peter. (Simon)
3. A famous mother-in-law. (Naomi)
4. One of the Patriarchs. (Isaac)
5. Ham's eldest son. (Cush)
6. A baby killer. (Herod)
7. A shepherd boy who became king. (David)
8. A pal of the king of beasts. (Daniel)
9. An unloved but prolific wife. (Leah)
10. A prophet whose message was love. (Hosea)
11. The first man. (Adam)

GEOGRAPHY GAME

Read the following list of countries and places to the players and ask them to write down their location. For instance: Peru is in South America, Manitoba is in Canada, etc. Here is the list:

1. Albania (Europe)
2. Alberta (Canada)
3. Andorra (Between France and Spain)
4. Bolivia (South America)

5.	Bulgaria	(Europe)
6.	Burma	(Asia)
7.	Costa Rica	(Central America)
8.	Estonia	(U.S.S.R.)
9.	Finland	(Europe)
10.	Honduras	(Central America)
11.	Guatemala	(Central America)
12.	Klondike	(Canada)
13.	Latvia	(U.S.S.R.)
14.	Madagascar	(Island off Africa)
15.	Morocco	(Africa)
16.	New Brunswick	(Canada)
17.	Nicaragua	(Central America)
18.	Ontario	(Canada)
19.	Paraguay	(South America)
20.	Rwanda	(Africa)
21.	Syria	(Asia)
22.	Tibet	(China)
23.	Turkey	(Asia)
24.	Venezuela	(South America)
25.	Yukon	(Canada)

The winner will be the one who locates most of these places correctly.

OBSERVATION GAME

Select a book from your library—preferably a novel of more than 300 pages—and pass it around to your guests to examine. Let each one give the book a thorough examination. Now, remove the book from sight and have the assembled company answer the following questions:

1. What is the title?
2. Who is the author?
3. Who is the publisher?
4. When was the book copyrighted?
5. How many pages are there in the book?

6. What color is the cover?
7. What edition is the book?
8. Where are the page numbers located?
9. How was it printed?
10. Who wrote the preface?

Of course, the one who gets the most correct answers is the winner.

SPELLING BEE NO. 1

Make as many copies of the following list of words as there are players and distribute one list to each. Some of these words are spelled incorrectly and some correctly. It is up to the players to determine which are incorrect and spell them correctly.

Here is the list:

1. exuberance	7. picknicking
2. accomodate	8. tarantula
3. laryngitis	9. oculist
4. apothesis	10. liquify
5. irascability	11. corruptible
6. idiocyncrasy	12. seizeable

ANSWERS

Words 1, 3, 4, 8, 9, and 11 are correct. The correct spellings of the other words are as follows: 2. accommodate; 5. irascibility; 6. idiosyncrasy; 7. picnicking; 10. liquefy; 12. seizable.

SPELLING BEE NO. 2

The directions to this one are the same as Spelling Bee No. 1.

Here's the list:

1. obfuscate
2. cuniform
3. rediculous
4. armadilo
5. tintinabulation
6. heretic
7. feret
8. cumulus
9. braggadocio
10. malicious
11. corolary
12. nauseous

ANSWERS

Words 1, 6, 8, 9, 10, and 12 are correct. The correct spellings of the other words are as follows: 2. cuneiform; 3. ridiculous; 4. armadillo; 5. tintinnabulation; 7. ferret; 11. corollary.

GUGGENHEIM

Select any five letter word and then print it horizontally on the paper. If the word is "candy," write "C" (leave a fair sized space), "A" (fair sized space), "N" (fair sized space), "D" (fair sized space), "Y" (fair sized space). At the side determine your categories, for instance you might have "flowers" for the first one, "cities" for the next, "poets" for the next, etc. These are to be written, one under the other, at the left hand margin. Now it is up to everyone to fill this in. He must think of a flower beginning with "C," one beginning with "A," one beginning with "N," etc. and write its name under each of these letters. Then he must start with cities—a city beginning with "C," one beginning with "A," etc. When he has written those, he must start with poets, and so forth, depending on how many categories you selected. Of course, the winner is the one who completes his diagram first.

There is another way of playing this, and that is to give special ratings on each name guessed. If there are ten people playing and they all get "Cleveland" for a city beginning with "C," each one can score one point, but if only one person has "Cleveland" he gets ten points. In this way odd names will be thought of in order to avoid repetition and the consequent loss of scoring.

	C	A	N	D	Y
flowers		aster		daisy	
cities	cleveland	albany	Newark	Detroit	Yonkers
poets				Dante	
musical instruments	clarinet			Drum	
diseases	catarrh				

SNAP JUDGMENT

This requires a little preparation on the part of the host or hostess. Cut out as many pictures from newspapers or magazines as you wish. The more you cut out, the longer will be the game. The pictures must be of well-known people—people who are constantly in the public eye. After you have clipped these pictures from the newspapers and magazines, cut off the names and give each a number. Paste them all on a board or lay them on the floor before your guests and let them identify the pictures. "Who is number ten?" "Who is number six?" "Number fourteen is very familiar, but I forget his name." You'll hear lots of comments and won't find many winners.

FINISH THE STORY

This is a hilarious game. The guests are seated in a circle. Each guest starts to write a story at the top of his paper. After he has written two or three sentences, it is up to you to cry

"Stop!" and tell everyone to fold his paper and pass it to his neighbor, who must not see what was previously written. At the word "GO!" everyone continues again to write two or three sentences, trying to be as funny as possible and with the idea in mind of trying to continue the thought of the first two sentences which cannot be seen. It is not necessary for each person to continue with the story which he has already started.

This goes on until the papers have been passed completely around the circle. They are then opened and read, and believe us, you will hear some mighty funny stories.

WHO IS GUILTY?

This is a real psychological game. There is no trickery or stunt connected with it. It should work every time and is based entirely on the laws of psychology.

The object is to find the guilty person, and the guilty person is the one who has read a certain sentence which you have written.

Send two people out of the room and, after they have left, write a sentence on a piece of paper and show it to the remaining guests. Now fold this piece of paper so that it is small enough to go into the palm of the hand and call in the two people who have left the room, instructing them as follows:

"I have written a sentence on this piece of paper and am going to give it to one of you. You are both to leave the room again, but *only one* of you must read what is on that paper, the other one must not see it, and we leave you on your honor to do this. After *one* of you has read this, and the *other has not*, both of you are to return."

While the two "suspects" are out of the room make up a list of twenty words, like "red," "chair," "Bible," etc.—any words that come into your head. Included in that list must be at least *eight synonyms or words suggestive of the words which were in the sentence.* For example, if the sentence contained the word "rose," your list would contain the word "red," which would naturally bring the reaction "rose" from the one who has *not* read the paper.

When the two "suspects" return, it is up to you to put each one through a series of word reactions. As you give the first "suspect" these words, watch his reactions carefully. He must give the first word that comes into his head, *as quickly as possible!* If you say "Red," he must instantly say the first word that pops into his head. If you say "Chair," he must say the first word that pops into his head. If he reacts quickly and unselfconsciously to the entire list, you may be sure he did *not* read the sentence. If, on the other hand, he pauses or becomes nervous when he hears a word which happened to be in the sentence, you will know that he is the "guilty person."

Of course, the sentence must not be an ordinary one though it should contain simple words.

As an example, let us suggest the sentence "All cows eat grass when they get a chance." When your "suspects" return, you will have a list, among which are included the words "bulls," "chew," "opportunity." The "suspect" who avoids saying "cow" when you say "bull," or who hesitates, is obviously the one who read the sentence. The other one will naturally say "cow." The same thing is true with the word "opportunity" which suggests the word "chance." The "guilty" one is the one who read the sentence, and your guests are the "jury."

TELEGRAMS

Tell your guests to write out the most appropriate telegram, the initial letter of each word of which shall form a given word. To illustrate, the author gave this game over the air during a presidential campaign, and asked for a sentence, the initial letter of each word of which would spell "President." As an example he gave the following sentence: *P*erhaps *R*oosevelt *E*xpects *S*uccess *I*n *D*emocratic *E*lection *N*ext *T*uesday. One of the prize-winning replies was: *P*icture *R*epublicans *E*ating *S*pinach *I*f *D*emocrats *E*njoy *N*ational *T*urkey.

You may choose any word you wish to give your guests, but be sure that the "telegrams" they write follow the rule and are appropriate. The funniest or most appropriate telegram wins.

CONFIDENCES

This game, old as it is, will always make a hit. Have your guests write the following at your direction:

1. Each boy writes a girl's name; each girl a boy's name. The names should be taken from among those present.
2. Now write the name of some place. Under this, write a date in the past.
3. Now write some slang expression, such as "and how" or "You're telling me," or some other expression meaning the extreme.
4. Now each boy writes a girl's name and each girl a boy's name, from among those present.
5. Put down three virtues or good qualities—exaggerate them as much as you like.
6. Put down three faults. The more slang you use, the better for this purpose.
7. Write down a number between one and one hundred.
8. Write down some word expressive of doubt, like "perhaps," "maybe," etc.

When everybody has done this, and numbered each item, read the following questions, and have each guest in turn read what is on his paper.

1. To whom did you make your first proposal? (Or who was the first man who proposed to you?)
2. Where, and when, did this happen?
3. Were you in love with one another?
4. Who else was interested in you at the time?
5. What do you consider your fiancé's best qualities?

6. What are his, or her, main faults?
7. How many children do you expect to have after you are married?
8. Do you think that you will be happy?

DRAWING CONTEST

Let each guest write the name of some familiar animal on a sheet of paper. Now collect these sheets and scramble them in a hat. Have each guest choose one of them, and, at a given signal, start to draw on the back of the page his conception of the animal whose name appears on his paper. Have each guest number his drawing, and then collect all of them again. Now lay all the drawings on the floor and have everyone write the name of each animal and its number. The guest who has identified the most animals correctly wins the game.

PROFILES

Arrange the players in a circle and have each one draw, to the best of his ability, the profile of the person on his right. Allow two minutes for this and then tell everyone to write the name of the person he just drew on the back of the paper and hand the paper to you.

After you have all the papers mix them up and rearrange them on the floor, face up. Now have each person try to pick out his own portrait. Needless to say there may be no winner of this game.

CONSEQUENCES

This game is a variation of CONFIDENCES and is always great fun. Here are the rules:

1. Each player writes down an adjective suitable for a girl, folds the paper over, and passes it to his neighbor, who cannot see what adjective is written.
2. Each player writes the name of a girl present, folds the paper, and passes it to his neighbor.
3. Now everyone writes the word "met," and after it, an adjective descriptive of some boy present (the funnier the adjective, the better it will be). The papers are then folded, passed, and the name of a boy who is present at the party is written down by each guest. Along with frequent foldings and passings, the guests should write "where they met," "what he said to her," "what she said to him," "what he gave her," "what she gave him," and "what everybody said about the affair."

The papers are now unfolded and each guest reads the complete story, which will be unusually funny.

YOU SEE BUT YOU DON'T OBSERVE

Tell your guests that you are going to mention twenty different articles which they see and handle every day of their lives, yet there is not one of them who can answer all the questions about these articles correctly. Of course there will be a great deal of guessing done and it is perfectly fair provided that they guess the right answer. Obviously, the winner will be the one who answers most of these questions correctly. Answers are at the end of this section.

1. Which way does the Jack of Hearts face? . . . .
2. Whose head is on the 5¢ stamp? . . . .
3. About how long is a king-size cigarette? . . . .
4. About how long is a dollar bill? . . . .
5. How many matches are there in an ordinary book of matches? . . . .
6. What are the dimensions of a piece of typewriting paper?
. . . .

7. Which way do you turn a radiator handle to turn the steam on? . . . .
8. How many prongs has a table fork? . . . .
9. What is pictured on the back of a $5 bill? . . . .
10. How wide is a newspaper column? . . . .
11. What are the colors of the auto license plates in your state? . . . .
12. How long is the standard make of writing pencil (approx.)? . . . .
13. Are the cutting edges of a pair of scissors straight or slightly curved? . . . .
14. Is there any dark blue in a match or candle flame? . . . .
15. Are the divisions on your radio dial all equal? . . . .
16. What kind of 6 is there on a man's wrist watch? . . . . . .
17. Is the postmark used to cancel the stamp? . . . .
18. On your telephone dial what letters are above the 4? . . . .
19. Is the coin return on a pay telephone on the right side? . . .
20. What color stripe is directly under the blue in our flag? . . . .

ANAGRAMS

Tell the players to write down the following words. They are to add to each word the letter which you give them to form a new word. The one who has the most words wins. Answers are at the end of this section.

1. S A F E with C
2. T A L E with R
3. T O R E with V
4. I D E A with S
5. G O R E with U
6. M A S H with E
7. C R A B with E
8. F L A R E with F
9. L I E D with Y
10. O U S T with G

11. P E S T with Y
12. V E A L with G
13. B E E T S with G
14. R I V E T with Y
15. W I V E S with L
16. R A N G E with D
17. A P P L E with A
18. R I S E N with D
19. A N G E R with T
20. O M E N S with G

BIOGRAPHIES

Before the guests arrive prepare a number of very short biographies of great people. Don't make them too long and don't give away too many details or you will spoil the story. Above all, don't be too vague. Here is a sample:

> This genius lived in the latter half of the 18th century and the beginning of the 19th. His life was a series of disappointments but in spite of it he rose to supreme heights and became a world figure who will live forever. He never married although he was in love a number of times. He was unattractive to look at and in his youth was uncouth. In his later years he became deaf.

HIS NAME WAS (Beethoven)

GUESSING GAME

This game requires no skill or knowledge—it is purely a matter of guessing.

Display a series of articles whose number or weight the guests must guess and record. One point is allowed for each article guessed correctly or nearly correctly, and the person who has the most points wins. Here is a suggestion for some displays:

1. The weight of a milk bottle (empty)
2. The number of pins in a small box
3. The length of a piece of string
4. The number of words on a particular page of a certain book
5. The number of pages in a closed book which anyone may select
6. The quantity of water in a kitchen pot
7. The number of cubic feet in the room

8. The number of yards in a long piece of thread
9. The weight of the host
10. The number of playing cards which you hold in your hand.

Be sure beforehand that you know the answers to all these. Be sure to weigh the empty milk bottle, count the number of pins that you place in the box, measure the length of the string, etc. You will avoid delay and argument by doing this ahead of time.

GENERAL QUIZ GAME

Read the following 20 questions to your family or friends and give them time to answer each one as you finish reading it. The winner will have the greatest number of answers correct. Answers are at the end of this section.

1. What is the capital of Montana?
2. Who wrote *Vanity Fair?*
3. When was the Treaty of Versailles signed?
4. Where is Trieste?
5. Why does a glass crack when you pour boiling water into it?
6. Which is correct: "none are here" or "none is here"?
7. Where was Lincoln born?
8. How much is the cube of three halves?
9. What is meant by a writ of Habeas Corpus?
10. Where is Peru with respect to Argentina?
11. What is a mantilla?
12. At what temperature is water at the maximum density?
13. What is a piccolo?
14. Who won the World Series in 1936?
15. How many players are there on a Cricket team?
16. Where does chicle come from?
17. What is a G man and how did he get that name?
18. Where is the nadir?
19. Who ran against Coolidge in 1924 for the Presidency?
20. About how high is Mount Everest?

Of course you may make up as many more questions as you choose or vary this game as you see fit.

QUESTION AND ANSWER

Give everybody two slips of paper, on the *first* of which each writes any question at all, afterwards writing any word at all on the *second* slip. Now collect all the questions in one bundle and all the words in another. Shuffle each bundle and then hand out to each player one question, one word paper, and a blank slip. Each player must now write on the blank slip an adequate answer to the question and in his answer he must use the word on his other paper.

SCRAMBLES

Prepare the following list and, instead of giving the names straight, scramble up the letters in the names as indicated. You may make up any list you wish but the following is a suggestion.

1. S P A N E L—The name of a city in Europe (Naples)
2. U O S H N D—The name of a river in America (Hudson)
3. L I E C H—The name of a country in South America (Chile)
4. R O G A K O N A—The name of an animal in Australia (kangaroo)
5. E R U I T P J—The name of a planet (Jupiter)
6. R E T A S—The name of a flower (aster)
7. P E A L P—The name of a fruit (apple)
8. M A T O O T—The name of a vegetable (tomato)
9. W A S P O R R—The name of a bird (sparrow)
10. T U E L F—The name of musical instrument (flute)
11. L O W L E Y—The name of a color (yellow)

12. C R U S E P—The name of a tree (spruce)
13. R A I I D H P H T E—The name of a disease (diphtheria)
14. V I R E N A M—The name of a goddess (Minerva)
15. P E R C E—The name of a fabric (crepe)
16. P N A I M U L T—The name of a metal (platinum)
17. D R E A M L E—The name of a precious stone (emerald)
18. C A T E M B H—The name of a great tragedy (Macbeth)
19. R U S E O P R I—The name of a lake in America (Superior)
20. O M E Y O E R T U D N—The name of a book in the Bible (Deuteronomy)

Give each player a copy of the list and, at the word "GO," tell them to unscramble the words. The one who has the most correct words wins.

DOUBLE DEALING

The object of this game is to list 24 words (not proper names) alphabetically (the letters *Q* and *J* are omitted) according to their double letters instead of their initial letters. The players are asked to write a word containing a double *a*, then a word containing a double *b*, then a word containing a double *c*, and so on all through the alphabet. The double letters must be in the word and they may begin it, but they may *not* end it. The word *address* could be listed under *d* but not under *s*, the word *settee* could be listed under *t* but not *e*.

Some words are almost too easy while others seem impossible. It is nothing to write a word with double *t* in it, but it is extremely difficult, if not impossible, to write a word with double *y* in it.

The game is played for high score, each letter scoring according to the list below:

double a	4		double n	1
" b	1		" o	1
" c	1		" p	1
" d	1		" r	1
" e	1		" s	1
" f	1		" t	1
" g	2		" u	7
" h	7		" v	10
" i	4		" w	15
" k	5		" x	15
" l	1		" y	15
" m	1		" z	3

The highest possible score is 100 and the par is 1. When the players have finished, have each one read his list and give him the correct point values according to the above table. The highest score wins.

Here is a score of 85 which is about as high as anyone can ever get:

*aa*rdvark	ski*i*ng	new*s*stand
bu*b*ble	boo*kk*eeper	si*t*ting
a*cc*ept	fa*ll*en	vac*uu*m
ru*dd*er	ru*mm*age	fli*vv*er
fe*e*ding	ru*nn*ing	po*ww*ow
co*ff*in	st*oo*p	e*xx*ray man *
da*gg*er	a*pp*ear	ja*zz*ing
high*h*and	a*rr*est	

ANSWERS

YOU SEE BUT YOU DON'T OBSERVE

1. To the right
2. George Washington
4. 6⅛ inches
3. 3¼ inches

* An xray man who lost his job.

5. 20
6. 8½ by 11 inches
7. To your left (counter-clockwise)
8. 4
9. The Lincoln Memorial
10. 2 inches
11.
12. 7½ inches

13. slightly bent
14. Yes
15. No
16. There is usually no 6 there
17. Sometimes
18. G H I in New York
19. Left
20. White

ANAGRAMS

1. Cafés
2. Later
3. Voter
4. Aside
5. Rouge

6. Shame
7. Brace
8. Raffle
9. Yield
10. Gusto

11. Types
12. Gavel
13. Begets
14. Verity
15. Swivel

16. Garden
17. Appeal
18. Diners
19. Garnet
20. Gnomes

GENERAL QUIZ GAME

1. Helena
2. Thackeray
3. June 28, 1919
4. Italy
5. The outside of the glass does not expand as quickly as the inside
6. None is here
7. Hardin County, Kentucky
8. 3⅜
9. An order to produce the body
10. Northwest
11. Spanish lace cape, worn by women
12. 4 degrees centigrade
13. A small musical instrument
14. Yankees
15. 11
16. Bully tree or the sapodilla

17. Government detective
18. Point directly down in the opposite direction from the zenith, which is directly overhead
19. John W. Davis
20. 29,000 feet

QUIZ GAMES

MODERN QUIZ GAMES

The following quiz games should be played by volunteers. Call upon five or six people to come up and face the audience while you fire these questions at them. A scorekeeper keeps accurate score of their answers.

If Jones fails to answer a question correctly or completely, then Smith must answer that question correctly or add to it to make it complete. If Smith can't do this it is up to the next person, and so on. *One question must be correctly or completely answered before the next question is asked.*

Each correct answer scores 10 points for the player answering it. Each incomplete answer scores 5 points. Every answer that goes toward completing a previous answer scores 5 points if it completes that answer. If it doesn't complete the answer, it scores zero. Incorrect or incomplete answers score zero and if nobody can answer a question correctly or completely it may be put up to the audience. If nobody in the audience can answer it correctly or completely, then each volunteer loses 2 points. The scorekeeper must keep accurate score and, of course, the one with the highest score wins the quiz and should get a prize.

Each quiz consists of ten questions with answers given after each question for your convenience in conducting these quizzes. In most cases there are many more correct answers to the questions than those given, and if anyone gets an answer that is not in the book, it is up to you and the audience to decide on the correctness of that answer and act accordingly.

Of course these quizzes may be played as written games.

GENERAL QUIZ I

1. Name eight slang expressions in which an article of clothing is mentioned.

ANSWERS

You're talking through your hat.
Hot under the collar.
Handle with kid gloves.
You bet your boots.
A kick in the pants.
A sock in the eye.
Shake in your shoes.
Takes the shirt off your back.
Keep it under your hat.
A bee in your bonnet.
Keep your shirt on.
Tied to your mother's apron strings.
High hat.
Something up his sleeve.
On the cuff.

2. Identify the following:

1. Dodo   4. Tom-tom
2. Dumdum   5. Yo-yo
3. Toto   6. Yum-Yum

ANSWERS

1. An extinct bird.
2. A kind of bullet.
3. The total. A famous clown.
4. A drum used by Indians.
5. A toy.
6. The heroine of the opera *Mikado*.

3. Mention ten trios of words that are associated together, viz: Red, white and blue.

ANSWERS

Wine, woman and song.
Sun, moon and stars.
Ready, set, go.
Knife, fork and spoon.
Hook, line and sinker.
Man, woman and child.
Lock, stock and barrel.
Faith, hope and charity.
Stop, look and listen.
Morning, noon and night.
Tom, Dick and Harry.
Deaf, dumb and blind.
Healthy, wealthy and wise.
Fair, fat and forty.
Hop, skip and jump.
Reading, writing and 'rithmetic.
Ear, nose and throat.
Going, going, gone.
Ready, willing and able.

4. Name fifteen states that end in the letter A.

ANSWERS

Alabama.
Alaska.
Arizona.
California.
Florida.
Georgia.
Indiana.
Iowa.

Louisiana.
Minnesota.
Montana.
Nebraska.
Nevada.
North Carolina.
South Carolina.
North Dakota.

South Dakota.   Virginia.
Oklahoma.   West Virginia.
Pennsylvania.

5. Where would you look for the following things? (Get 5.)

   1. A gantry.   5. A niblick.
   2. A bushing.   6. A vernier.
   3. An analama.   7. A lathe.
   4. A davit.   8. A pipette.

ANSWERS

   1. Over a number of railroad tracks.
   2. On a vehicle or in a machine shop.
   3. On a geographical globe.
   4. On a ship holding up a life boat.
   5. In a golf supply store.
   6. On a surveyor's transit.
   7. In a machine shop.
   8. In a chemical laboratory.

6. Name the following metals in order of their weights—the heaviest metal first:
   Copper, gold, osmium, lead, iron, platinum, aluminum.

ANSWERS

Osmium, platinum, gold, lead, copper, iron, aluminum.

7. Mention six different subjects taught in school or college which end in *ics*.

ANSWERS

Civics, calisthenics, economics, eugenics, ethics, dramatics, mechanics, mathematics, physics.

8. Name four well known books with colors in their titles.

ANSWERS

The Green Hat, The Mauve Decade, The Red & The Black, The Scarlet Letter, Study in Scarlet, So Red the Rose, Green Mansions, How Green Was My Valley, Dorian Grey, Tom Brown's School Days, A Clockwork Orange.

9. You arrive in a city in South America at noon on March 21st and you notice that the sun is directly overhead and there are no shadows. Where are you?

ANSWER

Quito, Ecuador. It is on the Equator.

10. The following definitions give the names of things which are similarly named in the human body, viz.: A musical instrument is a DRUM . . . ear DRUM. In each case the correct word is the second of a pair of words.

    1. An article of wearing apparel.
    2. A piece of cutlery.
    3. Hardware.
    4. A ship.
    5. A place of confinement.
    6. A seed.
    7. A kind of whip.
    8. It is used with tobacco.

ANSWERS

1. Knee CAP.
2. Shoulder BLADE.
3. Finger NAILS.
4. Blood VESSEL.
5. Brain CELL.
6. Arm PIT.
7. Eye LASH.
8. Wind PIPE.

GENERAL QUIZ 2

1. The initial letters of the last names of nine different Presidents spell the word PARAGRAPH. Name the presidents.

ANSWER

Pierce, Adams, Roosevelt, Adams, Grant, Roosevelt, Arthur, Polk, Hoover. (There are other names that will fit too.)

2. What do the following people do for a living? (Get 6.)

1. A cooper.
2. A millwright.
3. An actuary.
4. A sand hog.
5. A mendicant.

6. An impresario.
7. A taxidermist.
8. A pediatrician.
9. An orthodontist.
10. An osteopath.

ANSWERS

1. Makes barrels.
2. Works in a mill.
3. An insurance statistician.
4. Digs tunnels.
5. Begs.
6. Conducts or manages operas or concerts.
7. Stuffs animals.
8. A specialist in children's hygiene.
9. A dentist who specializes in teeth irregularities.
10. A manipulator of muscles and bones in treatment of certain diseases.

3. Mention six articles whose names are those of living creatures, viz: a baseball *bat*.

ANSWERS

Tailor's *goose*, Workman's *horse*, Lathe *dog*, Stop *cock*, *Pony, Mules, Skate, Fly,* Badminton *bird, Seal, Cat.*

4. Name seven medical terms ending in *itis*.

ANSWERS

Appendicitis, arthritis, bronchitis, carditis, laryngitis, meningitis, neuritis, peritonitis, sinusitis, tonsillitis, encephalitis, endocarditis, enteritis.

5. What eight states does Tennessee touch?

ANSWER

Kentucky, Virginia, North Carolina, Georgia, Alabama, Mississippi, Arkansas and Missouri.

6. List eight ways of spelling the sound O and give examples.

ANSWERS

O as in g*o*. Ow as in sn*ow*. Ough as in d*ough*. Ew in s*ew*. Eau as in b*eau*. Oe as in t*oe*. Ot as in jab*ot*. Oh as in *oh*. Oa as in b*oa*t. Owe as in *owe*.

7. What are the dates of the following?
   1. Twelfth night.
   2. Watchnight.
   3. Midsummer day.
   4. The Ides of March.

ANSWERS

1. The evening of January 6th.
2. New Year's Eve.
3. June 24th.
4. March 15th.

8. Mention five different kinds of cloth that begin with the five letters in CLOTH.

ANSWER

Calico, Linen, Organdy, Taffeta, Homespun.

9. Name the 18 (mainland) American republics.

ANSWER

Argentina, Bolivia, Brazil, Chile, Colombia, Costa Rica, Ecuador, El Salvador, Guatemala, Honduras, Mexico, Nicaragua, Panama, Paraguay, Peru, United States of America, Uruguay, Venezuela.

10. What is the unit of currency in the following countries? (Get 5.)

1. Holland.   5. Japan.
2. Switzerland.   6. China.
3. Italy.   7. Canada.
4. Spain.   8. Mexico.

ANSWERS

1. Guilder.   5. Yen.
2. Franc.   6. Yuan.
3. Lira.   7. Dollar.
4. Peseta.   8. Peso.

GENERAL QUIZ 3

1. Mention ten common first names of men and women that could be used as verbs, viz: Ward—to ward off a blow.

ANSWERS

Mark, Bob, Bill, Frank, Sue, Harry, Hope, Don, Rob, Jack, Will, Peg, Grace, Sally, Grant, Marshal, Page, Peter, Read, Wade, Jimmy.

2. Name six countries whose flags are red, white and blue.

ANSWERS

United States of America, England, France, Australia, Burma, Chile, Cuba, Liberia, Luxemburg, New Zealand,

Norway, Czechoslovakia, Yugoslavia, Iceland, The Netherlands, Panama.

3. For what are the following instruments used? (Get 5.)

1. Anemometer.	6. Hydrometer.
2. Barometer.	7. Iconometer.
3. Bolometer.	8. Micrometer.
4. Clinometer.	9. Radiometer.
5. Comptometer.	10. Thermometer.

ANSWERS

1. Measures wind pressure.
2. Measures atmospheric pressure.
3. Measures minute quantities of heat.
4. Measures angle of slope of hills.
5. Adds, subtracts, multiplies and divides.
6. Measures specific gravities.
7. Measures objects at a distance.
8. Measures thousandths of an inch.
9. Measures intensity of radiation.
10. Measures temperature.

4. What happened to the following Mother Goose characters?

1. The little mouse under the chair.
2. Peter, Peter, pumpkin eater's wife.
3. Solomon Grundy on Thursday.
4. Mother Hubbard's dog.
5. Miss Muffet.

ANSWERS

1. It was frightened by the pussy cat.
2. She was put in a pumpkin shell.
3. He took ill on Thursday.
4. It had to go without a bone.
5. She was frightened away by the spider.

5. Who invented the following? (Get 4.)

    1. The linotype.
    2. The automobile.
    3. The motion picture projector.
    4. The adding machine.
    5. The air brake.
    6. The fountain pen.
    7. The phonograph.
    8. The radio vacuum tube.

ANSWERS

    1. Mergenthaler.
    2. C. E. Duryea.
    3. Edison.
    4. Burroughs.
    5. Westinghouse.
    6. Waterman.
    7. Edison.
    8. de Forest.

6. Which of the following travel on land and which travel on water?

    1. A curricle.   4. A catamaran.
    2. A galleass.   5. A corvette.
    3. A barouche.   6. A brougham.

ANSWERS

    1. Land.   4. Water.
    2. Water.   5. Water.
    3. Land.   6. Land.

7. Name ten cities in the world with a population over 200,000, beginning with the letter B.

ANSWERS

Bagdad.   Baltimore.
Baku.   Bangalore.

Bangkok.	Bordeaux.
Barcelona.	Boston.
Belfast.	Bradford.
Belgrade.	Bremen.
Berlin.	Brisbane.
Birmingham (Eng.).	Bristol.
Birmingham (Ala.).	Brussels.
Bochum.	Bucharest.
Bogotá.	Budapest.
Bologna.	Buenos Aires.
Bombay.	Buffalo.

8. Name six symbols and superstitions that signify good luck and six that signify bad luck.

ANSWERS

Good Luck: Horseshoe. Four leaf clover. Wishbone. Black cat. Rabbit's foot. White horse. Spider. Picking up pins. Putting on garments inside out. Looking over your shoulder at the new moon.
Bad Luck: Number 13. Opal. Breaking a mirror. Walking under a ladder. Lighting three cigarettes on one match. Opening an umbrella in the house. Sitting 13 at the table. Getting out of bed the wrong side. Black cat crossing your path.

9. Name five states whose capitals are names of famous men.

ANSWERS

Michigan—Lansing.
Mississippi—Jackson.
Missouri—Jefferson City.
Nebraska—Lincoln.
North Carolina—Raleigh.
North Dakota—Bismarck.
Ohio—Columbus.
Wisconsin—Madison.

10. What are the most usual colors of the following gems?

1. Aquamarine.   5. Kunzite.
2. Topaz.   6. Carnelian.
3. Lapis Lazuli.   7. Amethyst.
4. Carbuncle.   8. Garnet.

ANSWERS

1. Blue or blue-green.   5. Lilac.
2. Yellow.   6. Red-orange.
3. Blue.   7. Purple.
4. Red.   8. Red.

GENERAL QUIZ 4

1. From what sources are the following things obtained and
   what are they used for? (Get 6.)

1. Snuff.   5. Isinglass.
2. Tapioca.   6. Caviar.
3. Asbestos.   7. Rouge.
4. Chicle.   8. Junket.

ANSWERS

1. Pulverized tobacco. Used to produce sneezing.
2. From the cassava plant. Used for food.
3. From the minerals amphibole or serpentine. Used for
   fireproofing.
4. The juice of the fruit from the sapodilla tree. Used in
   chewing gum.
5. Mica, also the viscera of fish. Used in electrical work.
6. The roe of sturgeon or other fish. A delicacy.
7. Oxide of iron. Used for cosmetics.
8. From curds, the coagulated part of milk. A food.

2. What horn cannot be blown, what tree cannot be climbed
   and what tongue never tasted food—all belonging to the
   same "family"?

ANSWER

A shoe horn, a shoe tree and the tongue of a shoe.

3. Identify the following:

   1. Bingo.   4. Jingo.
   2. Dingo.   5. Lingo.
   3. Ginkgo.

ANSWERS

1. Bingo is a game similar to lotto.
2. Dingo is a wild dog.
3. Ginkgo is a tree.
4. Jingo is a person who boasts about his country's ability to fight.
5. Lingo is language or dialect.

4. Name ten fruits and vegetables commencing with the letter *P*.

ANSWERS

Papaw, parsley, parsnip, pea, peach, peanut, pear, pepper, persimmon, pickle, pineapple, plum, pomegranate, potato, prune, pumpkin.

5. By changing the middle letter of a man's name I get a girl's name. What are the names?

ANSWER

Ira—Ida.

6. Name six games ending in BALL.

ANSWERS

Baseball, basketball, blowball, boxball, dodgeball, fieldball, football, handball, punchball, skeeball, tetherball, touchball, volleyball.

7. Mention seven common two-word expressions, one word of which is the name of a month, viz.: June bride.

ANSWERS

March winds, March hare, April shower, April fool, May queen, May apple, May blossom, May basket, May fly, June bug, June peas, June grass, September morn, October ale. (*Note:* Mayflower, Maypole, etc., are one word and do not count.)

8. Name the following canals in order of their length, the longest first.
Panama, Suez, Kiel, Cape Cod, Baltic–White Sea.

ANSWER

Baltic-White Sea, Suez, Kiel, Panama, Cape Cod.

9. Name the nine planets in order of their distance from the sun—the nearest one first.

ANSWER

Mercury, Venus, Earth, Mars, Jupiter, Saturn, Uranus, Neptune, and Pluto.

10. Name seven Mother Goose poems which commence with the same word or words repeated, viz.: Mary, Mary, quite contrary.

ANSWERS

Peter, Peter, pumpkin eater.
Tom, Tom, the piper's son.
Pat-a-cake, Pat-a-cake, baker's man.
To market, to market to buy a fat pig.
Hark, hark, the dogs do bark.
Pussy cat, pussy cat, where have you been?
Barber, barber, shave a pig.
Baa, Baa, black sheep.
Goosie, Goosie gander.

GENERAL QUIZ 5

1. Define ten of the following slang words or expressions:

   1. Canal boats.
   2. A china closet.
   3. A dicer.
   4. Ice.
   5. A lottery ticket.
   6. Bread.
   7. Tears.
   8. Tin cow.
   9. A dip.
   10. A doormat.
   11. A grand.
   12. Misplaced eyebrow.
   13. Pie-wagon.
   14. Paperhanger's daughter.

   ### ANSWERS

   1. Large shoes.
   2. Set of false teeth.
   3. A high hat.
   4. A diamond.
   5. A marriage license.
   6. Money.
   7. Onions.
   8. Condensed milk.
   9. A pickpocket.
   10. A coward.
   11. $1000.
   12. A mustache.
   13. Police wagon.
   14. A wall-flower.

2. The initial letters of six world famous rivers, each in a different country, spell the word STREAM. Name the rivers.

   ### ANSWER

   St. Lawrence, Thames, Rhine, Euphrates, Amazon, Mississippi. (There are other correct answers.)

3. What are the first names of the following Old Masters? (Get 4.)
   1. Van Dyck. 2. Mozart. 3. Sargent. 4. Schumann. 5. Van Gogh. 6. Beethoven. 7. Tchaikovsky. 8. Rubens.

   ### ANSWERS

   1. Anthony. 2. Wolfgang. 3. John. 4. Robert. 5. Vincent. 6. Ludwig. 7. Petr. 8. Peter.

4. What two vegetables begin and end with the same two letters in the same order?

ANSWER

Onion, tomato.

5. What would you boil by putting it on a cake of ice?

ANSWER

Liquid air (or other gas).

6. Name three famous books whose titles contain the words CITY, TWO CITIES, and THREE CITIES, respectively.

ANSWER

The Voice of the City (O. Henry).
A Tale of Two Cities (Charles Dickens).
Three Cities (Sholem Asch).

7. Name the President who preceded and followed:

1. Harding.   4. Monroe.
2. Harrison (Benjamin).   5. Hoover.
3. Lincoln.   6. F. D. Roosevelt.

ANSWERS

1. Wilson, Coolidge.
2. Cleveland, Cleveland.
3. Buchanan, A. Johnson.
4. Madison, J. Q. Adams.
5. Coolidge, F. D. Roosevelt.
6. Hoover, Truman.

8. What is the shape of the area that I get if I cut the following solids in half vertically, horizontally and slantingly:

1. Cone. 2. Cylinder. 3. Pyramid. 4. Sphere.

ANSWERS

1. Triangle, circle and ellipse.
2. Oblong, circle and ellipse.
3. Triangle, square and trapezoid.
4. Circle, circle and circle.

9. Name 5 famous composers of opera whose last names end in *i*.

ANSWER

Bellini, Cherubini, Cui, Ponchielli, Rossini, Donizetti, Mascagni, Puccini, Verdi, Wolf-Ferrari.

10. Name five citrus fruits.

ANSWER

Citrange, citron, grapefruit, lemon, lime, mandarin, kumquat, orange, shaddock, tangelo, tangerine.

SCIENCE QUIZ

1. Why does:
    1. Blotting paper absorb ink?
    2. An airplane rise into the air?
    3. The sun and rain produce a rainbow?

ANSWERS

1. The tiny fibers of the paper act as little lamp wicks, sucking up the ink by capillary action.
2. The wings are curved on top and flat on the bottom. This curve causes the air to rush past more rapidly on the top of the wing than on the bottom and this rushing air produces a lower pressure at the top so that the normal pressure on the bottom pushes the wings and the plane up.

3. Each little drop reflects and refracts the sun's light. The refraction or bending produces color which is reflected down to the observer. The particular color depends upon the angle from which the drops are seen. All drops passing a certain angle are red. All drops passing another angle are green, etc.

2. Name seven common elements that go to make up the word THOUGHT by naming a common element beginning with *T*, a common element beginning with *H*, etc.

ANSWER

Tin, Hydrogen, Oxygen, Uranium, Gold, Helium, Tungsten.

3. Here are seven metals. Name them in the order in which they conduct heat and electricity, the best conductor first.

   1. Steel.   5. Copper.
   2. Nickel.   6. Lead.
   3. Silver.   7. Gold.
   4. Aluminum.

ANSWERS

   1. Silver.   5. Nickel.
   2. Copper.   6. Steel.
   3. Gold.   7. Lead.
   4. Aluminum.

4. Give two proofs that, unlike most liquids, water *expands* when it freezes.

ANSWER

   1. The bursting of water pipes in very cold weather.
   2. The fact that ice is lighter than water.

5. In the United States the full moon is high in the sky in winter and low in the sky in summer. Why is this?

ANSWER

The full moon is always opposite the sun, or nearly so. Being close to the Ecliptic or path of the sun, it is about where the sun would be six months hence. On June 21st the full moon will be approximately where the sun is on December 21st and on December 21st it will be approximately where the sun is on June 21st.

6. How is Easter Sunday determined?

ANSWER

It is the first Sunday after the first full moon after the vernal equinox (March 21st).

7. Two cannon balls, each weighing 10 pounds, are sent away from the top of a 200 foot tower. The first ball is shot horizontally and it travels 7 miles before it hits the ground. The other ball is merely dropped. It travels only 200 feet. which ball hits the ground first and why?

ANSWER

They both hit the ground at the same time. No matter where the first ball is or how far away it is, it is 16 feet below the top of the tower at the end of the first second. At the end of the second second it is 64 feet below the top of the tower, no matter how far it has traveled from the tower. The same, of course is true for the dropped ball. Both balls, therefore, fall *vertically* with the same speed.

8. A prime number is any number that is not divisible by any other number except 1 and itself. 17 is a prime number because the only numbers that will go into it evenly are

1 and 17. Other prime numbers are 19, 23, 37, and 41. Can you name a prime number that is *not* an odd number?

ANSWER

2 is the only even prime number.

9. Why do the planets keep on revolving about the sun century after century without slowing down to any noticeable degree?

ANSWER

Because of the law of inertia. All bodies will keep going forever unless stopped by some outside force. Friction stops bodies on the earth but in the vast spaces of the Solar System there is no friction and hence nothing to stop the planets.

10. Suppose you took an expedition to the North Pole in the summer. How would you know that you were at the pole?

ANSWER

The sun makes a complete circle around the horizon in a day, never getting any higher or any lower in the sky.

LAZY LETTERS QUIZ

This quiz has to do with silent letters in words. What, for example, is the use of the *b* in *lamb* or the *p* in *pneumonia*? As some of these questions are difficult to answer it might be well to put the entire quiz up to the audience instead of calling up volunteers. Just call for a show of hands and rate the players according to the number of words they get right. If nobody gets a particular question, you will have to give the answer and go to the next question.

1. Mention another word, besides *doubt,* in which the *b* is silent.
   ANSWER: debt, subtle.

2. Mention another word beside *czar* in which the *c* is silent.
   ANSWER: indict.

3. Can you name any word without double letters in which a *d* is silent?
   ANSWER: Wednesday.

4. Mention another word beside *gnu* in which the *g* is silent at the beginning, and another word beside *design* in which the *g* is silent in the word.
   ANSWER: gneiss, phlegm.

5. Mention another word beside *rhinoceros* in which the *h* is silent in the word.
   ANSWER: ghost.

6. Can you name any word in which the *i* is silent?
   ANSWER: plaid.

7. Name a word in which a *q* is not followed by a *u.*
   ANSWER: Iraqis.

8. Can you name a word in which an *m* is silent?
   ANSWER: mnemonics.

9. Name a word in which the *p* is silent at the beginning of the word and another word in which *p* is silent *in* the word.
   ANSWER: psalm, receipt.

10. What common word makes the letter *o* sound like the letter *i*?
    ANSWER: women.

AMERICAN FLAG QUIZ

The author recently conducted a survey to see how many Americans knew what their flag looks like. The results of this survey were amazing. Out of one hundred people, picked at random, who were asked to draw Old Glory from memory, only one—an ex-army officer—drew the flag correctly! All the rest put in too many stripes or too many stars or did something else wrong. In view of this it would be well to pass out papers to everyone and ask to have the American Flag drawn from memory. It is a safe bet that not more than one person in the entire crowd will draw it correctly. Try it and see.

When you have finished the flag drawing game start on the Flag quiz. This should be conducted like any other quiz game. Pass out paper and read each question slowly and allow time to write down the answers. When all questions have been read, give the answers and let the players mark their own papers.

Here is the quiz:

1. How many stripes did the original Star-Spangled Banner have? How many red stripes?
   ANSWER: 15. 8 red.

2. Who designed the first American Flag?
   ANSWER: Nobody knows. It was *not* Betsy Ross.

3. How long should the flag be displayed?
   ANSWER: From sunrise to sunset.

4. When our flag is displayed with other flags which should be the highest?
   ANSWER: None. They all should be equal in height and size. (*U. S. Flag Association*)

5. How would you dispose of tattered, worn out flags?
   ANSWER: They should be burned.

6. What is the main thing to be careful of when lowering the flag?

    ANSWER: To keep it from touching the ground.

7. When the flag is displayed over the middle of a street which way should the blue field point?

    ANSWER: North or East.

8. What is the significance of the stars in our flag?

    ANSWER: Each star represents a state in the order in which it was admitted to the Union.

9. What should you do at a parade when the flag passes?

    ANSWER: Remove your hat and hold it with your right hand over your heart. If you are in uniform, stand at attention and salute.

10. Can the flag be used for anything other than display purposes?

    ANSWER: No.

GAMES FOR
SPECIAL OCCASIONS

SUGGESTIONS FOR DRESS-UP PARTIES

(Award a prize in each case for the best or funniest costume.)

FANCY DRESS FROM THE NECK UP

1. Evening dress from the neck down. The face must be covered and the masks or headgear must be in ridiculous contrast to the evening dress, for example: A giraffe's head on a tuxedo or a sunflower head on an evening dress.

HOBO PARTY

2. The men come as bums and hoboes. Have them wear their oldest clothes and not shave for a day or so, for the worse they look the better. The girls shouldn't fix their hair and should be in keeping with the appearance of the men. Welcome all guests at the back door and as they come in hand them a paper bag with a sandwich in it—just to give a little realism to the scene.

SUPPRESSED DESIRE PARTY

3. Each guest comes as his own particular suppressed desire. Whatever your desire is, try to picture it and come dressed as it.

SHIPWRECK PARTY

4. Each guest comes dressed as he would if he were in a ship-
   wreck late at night. The more hurriedly dressed they are,
   the better it will be.

CHILDREN'S PARTY

5. Each guest comes as a little child or even a baby.

CHARACTER PARTY

6. Each guest comes as a famous character in fiction or
   history.

IMPROVISED COSTUME PARTY

7. Each guest is given a newspaper, a scissors and a box of
   pins and told to make his or her own costume. Some crazy
   costumes will be worn—especially by the men.

LINCOLN'S BIRTHDAY

GETTYSBURG ADDRESS

When you are ready to play this game give each guest a
pencil and paper; tell them that you are going to read the
Lincoln Gettysburg Address to them but unfortunately it will
not be entirely complete. Every once in a while you will pause
and they are to write down the missing word or words. You will

tell them how many words are missing and as soon as they have written them down you will continue reading. The winner will be the one who has the greatest number of correct words on his paper.

Now slowly read the following, pausing at each blank to allow the guests to write in the missing word. In the second paragraph there are six words missing after the "Now we are . . ." Be sure to tell everyone that six words are missing before continuing with "testing whether that nation . . ."

This will be a lot of fun and you will be surprised how few people really know this famous masterpiece word for word.

Fourscore and seven years ago our fathers brought forth —— this continent a new nation, conceived in —— and dedicated to the proposition that all men are created equal.

Now we are —— —— —— —— —— ——, testing whether that nation or any nation so conceived and so dedicated can —— ——. We are —— —— —— —— —— of that ——. We have come to dedicate a portion of that —— as a —— —— —— of those who —— —— —— —— that that nation —— ——. It is altogether fitting and proper that we should do this.

But, —— —— —— ——, we cannot dedicate, we cannot ——, we cannot —— —— ——. The brave men, living and dead, —— —— ——, have —— it, far above our —— —— to add or ——. The world will little note, nor long remember, what we say here, but it can never forget what —— —— ——. It is for us the living, rather, —— —— —— —— to the —— —— which —— —— —— —— have thus —— —— —— ——. It is rather for us to —— —— —— —— the great task remaining before us—that from —— —— —— —— —— —— —— —— —— —— which they gave the last —— —— —— —— that we here —— —— that these dead shall not have died in vain— that this nation, under God, shall have a new birth of freedom—and that government of the people, by the people, for the people shall not perish from the earth.

WASHINGTON'S BIRTHDAY

WASHINGTON CROSSING THE DELAWARE

It is well known that when Washington crossed the Delaware he didn't have an easy time of it because of the large pieces of floating ice which hit against his small rowboat.

In honor of George, let one person at a time try to cross the room on paper icebergs in the following manner:

Place sheets of typewriter paper about 2 feet apart in a zigzag fashion from one end of the room to the other end. Number these sheets. Now call for a Washington and when he volunteers, tie his ankles together and start him on paper number 1. He is to hop from paper 1 to paper 2, then to 3, 4, 5, etc. until he reaches the other end of the room. He may be able to do it all right but it is also a question of speed and it is up to you to time him and record it. When he is finished the next volunteer tries and the one who crosses in the shortest time wins.

Be sure not to make it too difficult: don't have the papers too far apart and make the numbers on them clear and legible. You may place them anywhere you like and cover the entire room with them, just as long as they lead from one end of the room to the other and they are not too close together.

TRUTH

In honor of Washington the old game of Truth is particularly appropriate. This game is a lot of fun with a crowd who are willing to be good sports and not take offense. If you have any sensitive people at the party we advise you not to play this.

Make a list of the names of each person at the party at the left hand edge of a piece of paper and a list of characteristics above, as indicated in the diagram. As soon as this is done choose someone to rate and send him out of the room with instructions to rate himself exactly as he sees himself. He must tell the truth. When he has gone have everyone in the room rate him truthfully. Rating is done on a basis of ten.

Now call in the person who went out and have him read his opinion of himself to the crowd while you collect all papers and average up each item to strike a general average. When he is finished with his own rating, read your combined and average rating of him and see what the various differences are.

Make sure all guests have a turn.

	sex appeal	brains	beauty	sincerity	originality	sense of humor
Flo	6	7	4	9	2	4
Jack	3	9	1	10	5	7
May	9	1	9	9	0	2
Jerry	6	7	4	9	5	9
Kitty	8	7	8	10	7	9
Emily	4	8	4	9	3	6

ST. VALENTINE'S DAY

HEART THROBS

There are very few parties where one of the boys is not interested in one of the girls. As a rule everyone knows who John's girl friend is and whom Mary is crazy about.

Select a boy and a girl who are known to be sort of . . . well, you know . . . and have them sit facing one another. Now let each one hold the other's pulse and count the heart beats aloud without smiling or blinking or looking anywhere except into each other's eyes. Everyone else may laugh and talk as much as he wants but the valentine couple must be absolutely serious while they look into one another's eyes, feel each other's pulses and count out loud for two minutes.

If the valentine couple succeeds in doing their stunt you may be sure that they are pretty far gone on one another; if not, it's just a mild crush and nothing more.

LIMERICKS

Make up limericks for each of your guests and let them fill in the last line. This is much easier than it sounds and, with a little practice beforehand you will be able to do it very well. As you know a limerick must follow certain rules in regard to meter and rhyme and if you examine the following limerick you will see what we mean:

There was a young man who said "why
Can't I look through my ear with my eye?
    If I put my mind to it
    I'm sure I could do it
You never can tell till you try."

The first two lines and the last line rhyme. The 3rd and 4th lines are much shorter and rhyme.

You can begin all your limericks with

There was a young man (lady) named . . . .

and place the name of boy or girl in the blank.

Who loved a young lady (fellow) named . . . .

and place the name of the girl or the boy in the blank making sure that it rhymes with the first name. Now all you need do is write two short lines which rhyme and are funny and let one of your guests fill out the last line. Here is a typical limerick, assuming that there is a Jesse and a Bessie among your guests:

There was a young lady named *Bessie*
Who's sweet on a fellow named *Jesse*
It's easy to know
That wherever they go

. . . .

If you don't happen to have couples whose names rhyme you can use your ingenuity and rhyme a name with some other word, Harry, for example will rhyme with marry, Flora with adore her, Bert with flirt, etc.

Now make up as many different limericks as there are people at your party (one for each) and leave the last line out. When the guests arrive give each one a limerick and have them all fill out the last line. The best and funniest line wins.

ST. PATRICK'S DAY

BUBBLE BLOWING CONTEST

Supply each guest with a clay pipe tied with a green ribbon. Now produce a big bowl of soapy water and have each guest in turn come up and blow as large a bubble as he can, making a careful note of the winner. Now start over again and have each guest blow as small a bubble as he can and note the winner. The next is the highest bubble, then the most bubbles from one wetting of the pipe. The winners of each of these contests now compete in the finals and the winner of that is awarded a prize appropriate for St. Patrick's day.

KISSING THE BLARNEY STONE

Before the guests arrive prepare two flattering letters; one to one of the girls who is going to be at the party, and the other to one of the boys who will be there. These letters should be typewritten, if possible, and in case you want to save time thinking up what to say, you may copy the following two letters:

DEAR HELEN (or any other girl's name you choose)
I have the utmost respect and the highest admiration for your great intellect and unusual culture. You are one of the few girls who combines brilliant and sparkling wit with dignity and self-possession! Your attractive appearance is exceeded only by your remarkable personality. What is this fascination that you have over men that draws them to you in dozen lots like a magnet attracts carpet tacks? I have never seen anyone so beautiful and charming in my life for verily you have the mind of an Einstein behind the face of a Venus!

DEAR FRED (or any other boy's name you choose)
It is an honor to know you and to be considered one of your friends. Your marvelous physique, your manly strength and strikingly handsome face, coupled with your

great wisdom and dazzling mind sets my heart a-twitter when I am in your presence. You are model manhood personified—and I am only a mere girl who worships you like a god! What is the secret of your great success in life? What is this magnetism that you hold over all of womankind? How, in your early years did you acquire such a fund of knowledge and wisdom and why are you so extremely modest about it all? Perhaps it is because you rank with the world's outstanding men!

When the guests arrive, have a large flat piece of marble or slate on the table and call for a volunteer to "kiss the Blarney Stone." Call first for a boy and when he volunteers tell him that the old custom is to write his name while he is kissing the Blarney Stone. As soon as he bends over to kiss the stone, give him a pencil and tell him he must write his name without looking up while he is kissing the stone. He will do this, much to the amusement of the rest of the crowd. Of course you must substitute the letter which you wrote to the girl, folded in such a way as not to show any typing—it is to look like a blank piece of paper. What the boy is really doing is signing the letter, but he doesn't know it.

When the boy has finished kissing the Blarney Stone and writing his name, call for a girl to do the same thing. Of course there should be a lot of joking and kidding around to take everybody's mind off the real issue—the letters. The girl must do the same thing—she must write her name too, only this time you substitute the letter which you wrote to the boy.

Now, say nothing more about this and pretend that it is all over. Play some other game, but be sure to disappear, without anyone seeing you, sometime before refreshments are served and place the girl's letter in her place at the table and the boy's letter at his place at the table.

Imagine the surprise when both the girl and the boy sit down to the table and see these two ridiculously flattering letters signed by the two who kissed the Blarney Stone.

FOURTH OF JULY

THE STAR SPANGLED BANNER

How many Americans know all the words to the three stanzas of the *Star Spangled Banner?* The answer is very few, and because of this fact you can play an interesting game by having everyone stand up while you conduct the National Anthem. Of course you will have the words in front of you while you are leading your guests in song, but it is up to you, as soon as you see or hear anyone miss the lines, to make him about-face—turn his back to you.

The first stanza will be easy, since everyone knows it, but when you come to the second and third stanzas you will have to watch everyone carefully and be sure to have them turn their backs to you as soon as they make a mistake or stop singing the words.

The one who lasts the longest is the winner, but you may be pretty sure that before you finish the three stanzas everyone will have turned an about-face.

FLAG COLORING

Give each guest a pencil and paper and tell him to make a list of numbers from one to ten. The problem is to write after each number the colors of a particular flag. For instance, if you say, "One. What are the colors in the American Flag?" the obvious answer is, "Red, White and Blue." But that is too easy, so try the following:

1. The British Flag
2. The French Flag
3. The Italian Flag

 4. The Russian Flag
 5. The Chinese Flag
 6. The Japanese Flag
 7. The Swiss Flag
 8. The Greek Flag
 9. The Brazilian Flag
10. The Mexican Flag

HALLOWEEN

Perhaps Halloween parties are the most popular of all because Halloween has a definite tie-up with spooks and pranks and tricks. We will include in this section a general review of the various things that are done on Halloween. These are by no means new, yet we are suggesting them just as a sort of résumé of what has been done.

YOUR FORTUNE

Five soup plates are put next to one another on a table. The first one contains clear water, the second one soapy water, the third one a ring, the fourth one a little earth or talcum powder, and the fifth one nothing at all. Each guest is blindfolded and led to the table, where he must dip his finger into one of the soup plates. The contents of these plates mean the following:

1. Clear water means a happy marriage within the next five years.
2. Soapy water means an unhappy marriage within the next five years.
3. The ring means a proposal within the next three weeks.
4. The earth means a long journey within a month.
5. The empty soup plate means a marriageless, empty life.

STUNTS ON HALLOWEEN

The old stunt of ducking for floating apples in a big pan of water and trying to find a hidden penny with your mouth in a big dish of flour are well known and are always fun to do. Then there is the apple seed trick where the girl names five apple seeds after boys at the party. She wets these seeds and places them on her forehead. The first seed that falls off is the boy who is going to propose to her. There is also the mirror stunt which is to be played in a dark room with a candle. A girl approaches a medium-sized mirror (which is hung on a wall) with a lighted candle. The candle is the only light in the room and guests are standing all around. The first boy's face that the girl sees in the mirror will be her future husband. This can also be done with boys for their future wives.

THE GHOST'S RETURN

There are any number of stunts and tricks which are played over and over again on Halloween, most of which you undoubtedly know. They all have to do with fortune telling, crystal gazing or ghosts and spooks. Now we will give a new and original stunt which is sure to bring a thrill to your Halloween Party.

This is a grand trick and will give your guests the creeps. Have a dark seance with not more than 6 people seated around a light table—preferably a bridge table. The only light in the room must be centered on the table so that nobody cheats. The host is the medium and asks the spirits the questions. The spirits will answer through the table. If it tips once it means "YES" and if it tips twice it means "NO."

Now everyone is seated around the table and all hands must be placed flat on the table so the little finger of one hand is in contact with the thumb of the next hand. This will "complete the circuit." To add to all this, have everyone touch knees under the table—also "to complete the circuit." Now ask one of the people to get up and turn out the high lights and leave only the bridge lamp lit and near the table so that everyone can see that there is no trickery. As soon as this is done and the person who put the lights out returns to the table, the seance begins. The table will mysteriously tip once for YES and twice for NO after each question much to the horror of the guests!

How is it done? Very simple. The person who turns out the lights is in on the trick. He must be a man and must have a foot ruler concealed in his right sleeve. As soon as he comes back and takes his place at the table, he allows the ruler to project out a little and catch UNDERNEATH the table while his hand is innocently above the table. His sleeve is now the connecting link between his wrist and the ruler and if he moves his wrist he will tip the table easily without anyone knowing. This he does after every question.

MAGIC TRICKS

AN AMAZING PSYCHIC TRICK

This trick is one of the most baffling in all magic. Nobody will ever catch on to it and it will mystify everybody completely! It should be done by a man and wife or brother and sister or any two people who live together and can practice a little, though it is very simple. Here it is in its simplest form:

The girl leaves the room and someone takes a card and shows it to everyone in the room. The card is put back into the pack and the pack is shuffled thoroughly and put on a table face down. The girl comes in and guesses the card!

Suppose the 8 of Spades were chosen. It is put back into the pack and the pack is shuffled and put on the table. The girl enters and says:

"It's a black card"   You say "Yeah."
"It's a Spade"   You don't say anything.
"It is the 8 of Spades!"

This certainly seems unexplainable to everyone but it is extremely simple when you know how. Here is the clue:

The four edges of the table represent the four suits. Looking down at the table the upper edge is Spades, the right edge Hearts the lower edge Diamonds and the left edge Clubs. Of course the pack need not be placed way over at the edge but it *must* be placed enough off center to indicate the suit. In this case the pack is carelessly put over toward the "far" edge or the "top" of the table.

From now on it is just a question of memorizing 4 very simple things given in the following chart:

	YES	YEAH	YEP		NO ANSWER
YES	Ace	2	3	or	4
YEAH	5	6	7	or	8
YEP	9	10	J	or	Q
No answer at all to any question					King

From this table you can see that YES means one of four cards: Ace, 2, 3, 4, so if you answer YES the girl knows it is one of these cards. Your next answer will give the card since, if you look at each column, you will see YES, YEAH, YEP and NO ANSWER just as before. The 10, for example is YEP-YEAH, the 5 is YEAH-YES.

Now practice a little and see why these cards are what we say they are:

3 is YES-YEP
8 is YEAH-NO ANSWER
4 is YES-NO ANSWER
2 is YES-YEAH

NO ANSWER AT ALL TO ANYTHING .... King

As soon as the girl sees the position of the pack on the table she knows the suit. She then says:

"It's a black card" (this gives you a chance to say YES, YEAH, YEP or NOTHING AT ALL.)

You say YEAH.

"It's a Spade" (this gives you a chance for the second YES, YEAH, YEP or SILENCE.)

You say NOTHING.

The girl knows that YEAH-NO ANSWER is 8. She knew the suit as soon as she saw the table so she says:

"The 8 of Spades."

One more example: Suppose the 3 of Diamonds is picked.

The cards are put toward the *bottom* or *near edge* of the table as you face it. You know then that it is a Diamond. You then say:

"It's a red card," and your partner says "YES." This means that it is either the ace, 2, 3 or 4 of diamonds.

"It's a Diamond," and your partner says "YEP" which can only mean the 3.

You say, much to the amazement of all, "It's the 3 of Diamonds!"

A FEAT IN BALANCING

The next time you go to a party try this on the host—if he is a good natured soul—and watch the fun. Tell him that you heard that he was good at balancing things and get some girl that he has a crush on to ask him to balance a pan of water on a broomstick. Of course he'll say he can't but you show him how. Stand on a step ladder and hold a pan or a glass of water flat against the ceiling. Now ask your host if he can hold that pan or glass against the ceiling with a broom handle. Tell him it is quite a difficult stunt and get him anxious to show off. When he does do it and is standing on the ladder with the broom handle pressed against the bottom of the pan or glass, say to the other guests: "Fine, now let's go home. We've had a swell time, thanks," and pretend to leave him there and see what happens!

In case you do not want to take a chance with a glass or a bowl full of water balanced up against the ceiling, have your friend sit at a table with his hands out on the table, palms down. Now place a glass full of water on the back of each of his hands and tell him to balance these. When you have done this it is your cue to leave him alone and see what happens.

NAMING THE CARDS

Here is a fine old card trick that will mystify everyone who doesn't know it. Before you can do it you must learn a very simple short poem. This is the poem:

8 Kings threaten to save
95 Queens for 1 sick knave!

Say this over and over again until you know it thoroughly. Now look at the code:

8, King, 3, 10 (threaten) 2, 7 (save)
9, 5, Queen, 4, 1, 6, Jack (knave)

This includes the thirteen cards and all you need do is arrange the pack beforehand in that order, namely: 8, K, 3, 10, 2, 7, 9, 5, Q, 4, Ace, 6, J. As you do this be sure that the suits are: Spade, Heart, Diamond and Club.

Now put the pack face down on the table and say to everyone, "The first card that I will turn up is the 8 of Spades." Turn it up. "The next will be the King of Hearts" Turn it up. "The next will be the 3 of Diamonds" Turn it up. "The next will be the 10 of Clubs." Turn it up. "The next will be the 2 of Spades," etc.

You can go right through the pack this way and nobody will catch on to the trick.

A SIMPLE CARD TRICK

This trick can only be done with a pack of cards whose backs are not the same upside down as they are right side up. There are any number of packs like this—where pictures appear on the backs of the cards instead of designs. If you happen to have a pack of this description, all you need do is arrange all the cards so that the pictures are the same way. This is done, of course, before your guests arrive, or you can do it quickly, without anyone observing you, after they have arrived.

Form the pack into a fan shape and ask someone to take a card out. As soon as he has done this, even the pack up again and ask that person to look at his card and show it to everyone except you. Now, without anyone noticing, turn the pack of cards around in your hand so that when your friend puts the card he has chosen back into the pack it will be the only card *whose back is upside down*. When he has done this, you may shuffle the cards all you wish—it makes no difference, of course—and tell him that you will name his card.

Now, here is where the fun comes in! Holding the pack of cards in your left hand, with the backs up, and starting with the top card, go through the pack slowly, turning each card face up and noting that the picture on the back of each card is always in the same position. As soon as you come to a back which is upside down (the only back which is upside down in the whole pack), note what card it is when you turn it face up, *but say nothing about it.* Keep going for another five or six cards and then stop and say: "I will bet you five dollars that the next card I turn *over* will be your card." Of course, your friend will bet you because he has already seen his card passed over and you have said nothing about it. Everybody else in the room will bet you too, and think that you have missed out. When you are ready, all you need do is go back among the cards which are face up, pick up his card (which you know) and turn it over. You will win the bet.

To take an example, suppose your friend chooses the 10 of Diamonds. He puts it in the pack, and it is the only card whose back is upside down. As you go through the cards, turning each one face up, you come to the one that is upside down, and you notice when you turn it face up that it is the 10 of Diamonds. You say to yourself, "That is his card," but you keep on going just the same, without saying a word to anyone. After you have turned another five or six cards face up, stop and, remembering the 10 of Diamonds, inform everyone that the next card that you are going to turn over will be the chosen card. When everyone bets you, all you need do is go back and turn the 10 of Diamonds over.

CARD CODE TRICK

This is an old trick but not very well known. It is one of the most effective that we know of. It is done with 36 cards laid out face up in six squares of six cards each. Before you go out of the room, make sure that someone in the room understands the trick so that he can signal you, in an offhand manner. While you are out of the room, someone in the room selects one of the 36 cards without touching it. You come back and your confederate might say, as a passing remark to somebody in the room "I had chicken for lunch," which immediately will tell you that the card is the Ace of Hearts.

Now how does this work? It is extremely simple. The 36 cards are divided into the following categories in order:

1. Man   3. Beast   5. Fowl
2. Woman   4. Fish   6. Insect

The first six (3 columns of 2 cards each) have to do with man, the second six have to do with woman, the third six have to do with beast, the fourth six have to do with fish, the fifth six have to do with fowl, and the last six have to do with insects.

Each one of the six cards in each group is also divided into these categories, which makes it extremely simple. The second card in the first group is obviously MAN-WOMAN—so that if your confederate is a man he says, "I met Helen yesterday," you know it is MAN-WOMAN, the second card or the Queen of Clubs.

Your friend, in this case, says, "I had chicken for lunch," which means MAN-FOWL, placing the card as number 5 in the first group. Suppose your card were the second card in the fourth group (the 9 of Clubs), your confederate would then have to say something involving first a fish and then a woman.

He might say, "Sea bass never agrees with my wife." This immediately gives you the FISH-WOMAN combination.

Be sure that no one knows that your confederate knows anything about the trick. Make it appear as though he is merely entering into conversation with other people. The other guests will also make remarks, which you may disregard. You only pay attention to his first statement and get the combination immediately. You do not need to select the card right away. You can let other people talk before you do so, as this will add to the mystery of the trick.

MIND-READING

This is a mean trick—don't carry it too far. Test the various guests' psychic powers by sending several persons in turn out of the room, one at a time, while the entire group concentrates on some particular object. As each returns to the group and tries to guess what the object is, he will naturally fail, unless telepathy is more developed than we think it is; if he succeeds right off, it is quite spooky—but he won't. Having shown how poor the psychic qualities of these two or three guests are, you select some player who is good-natured and whom you wish to make the "goat." Make him leave the room and while he is out tell the crowd that whatever object he selects will be the one chosen. Have everyone agree to this. When he comes back, he will name an object, and everyone will marvel at his skill, congratulate him, and tell him how wonderful he is. Send him out again and let him miss one or two times before you all congratulate him, so that he won't get wise to the trick you are playing on him. If he were to succeed immediately two or three times in succession, he might catch on to the trick. Never let it go more than three questions. Everyone will have a good laugh, and the person who is the "goat" will think he is marvelous until he learns the secret.

CARD SPELLING

Select 13 cards, from the ace to the king inclusive, from a pack, and arrange them as follows: 3, 8, 7, ace, queen, 6, 4, 2, jack, king, 10, 9, and 5. This order should be memorized carefully. When you have the cards arranged thus, all you need do is spell them out, to the astonishment of your guests.

Holding this little pack in your left hand, take the top card, and without looking at it place it on the bottom and say "O." Now take the next top card and do the same thing, only this time say "N." Do the same with the next card and say "E."

Now *remove the next card* (which will be the ace), and you have O-N-E—1. When you put the ace on the table face up, say "one." Now continue just as you did before, spelling T-W-O— 2, but when you come to the card that should be two, throw it on the table face up, just as you did the ace, and say "two." Continue to spell T-H-R-E-E, always taking the top card and putting it underneath. After you have spelled three, the next card will be the three, which you throw down on the table face up. This continues until you have nothing but the king and queen in your hand. These cards go from top to bottom alternately as you spell Q-U-E-E-N and drop the queen face up as the next card. The last card, of course, will be the king.

TELEPHONE CARD TRICK

After the guests are all seated, take out a pack of cards from which all aces, 5's and 9's have been removed, and shuffle it thoroughly. Now ask anyone in the room to take a card and show it to everyone in the room. As soon as he does this tell him to go to the telephone and call up a certain number which you will give him and ask for Dr. so-and-so and he will tell what card was selected. This trick actually works!

Suppose one of your guests selects the 2 of Spades. After showing this card to everyone in the room he goes to the phone and, at your direction, calls Main 4725 and asks for Dr. Bates. As soon as "Dr. Bates" answers the telephone your friend says:

"Is this Dr. Bates?"
(*Voice at the other end of the phone*): "Yes."
"What card do I hold in my hand, Doctor?"
(*Voice*): "The 2 of Spades!"

Of course as many guests as care to, may witness this truly amazing telephone conversation to see that it is the real thing and no put-up job.

The trick is very simple. It is merely a code that you have with one or two friends who don't happen to be at the party. The vowels A, E, I, and O are the four suits in that order. A is

Spades, E is Hearts, I is Diamonds and O is Clubs. The face value of the card is the letter number in the alphabet (without vowels) for example:

```
1  2  3  4  5 6 7 8 9 10  J  Q  K
*  B  C  D  * F G H *  J  K  L  M
```

The first 2 letters of the doctor's name give the clue. The name, Dr. Bates, immediately told your friend at the other end of the phone (who knows this code) two letters: B and A. Now B stands for 2 and A is the Spade suit, therefore, the instant he heard "Dr. Bates?" he said to himself "2 of Spades."

It is up to you to make up these names as the cards are picked.

Here are a few examples:

Dr. Getton—7 of Hearts (GE)
Dr. Mole—King of Clubs (MO)
Dr. Jinks—10 of Diamonds (JI)

In case you live in a small town and there is a chance of someone in the room recognizing the phone number and yelling out, "That's not a doctor's phone number—that's Harry Smith's house," all you need do is arrange with your friend beforehand to be at the corner drug store at a certain time and wait at the pay telephone booth for your call. Then it is a simple matter if you know the number of the pay telephone in that drug store. Nobody will catch on because this number will not be familiar at all!

Be sure you remove all the aces, 5's and 9's from the pack before you do this trick.

BOY, WHAT A MEMORY!

Here is a wonderful memory trick which is sure to make everyone envious until he finds out how it is done!

Copy the following numbers on a piece of paper and tell your guests that a recent memory course has enabled you to memorize 50 of 100 different 10 digit numbers. This would be

146 · *The Big Book of Family Games*

a remarkable thing to do if it were legitimate so don't let anyone know how you do it and watch them gasp with admiration!
Here are a few of the numbers just to get you started—you can
work out the rest when you know the simple system. Work
them out up to 50 when you know the system.

1. 3145943707
2. 4156178538
3. 5167303369
4. 6178538190

5. 7189763921
6. 8190998752
7. 9101123583
8. 0224606628

Let anyone name any number and you will give the large
number opposite it. For example someone may say 27. You
think awhile and then say 9325729101. Someone may say 3.
You think awhile and then say 5167303369. Here is how it
works:

As soon as you hear the number mentally add 12 to it and
reverse the digits. Now mentally add these digits together and
place the result to the right as the next digit and so on. Take 3
for example. If you add 12 you get 15 and, reversing this you
get 51 which is the number you start off with. Now 5 + 1 is 6,
therefore 6 is the next digit. 6 + 1 is 7 and 7 is the next digit.
Now 7 + 6 is 13 so 3 is the next digit (disregard the 1). Now
3 + 7 is 10 so 0 is the next digit (disregard the 1). 3 + 0 is 3
which is the next digit, 3 + 3 is 6 which is the next digit and
3 + 6 is 9 which is the last digit!

Here is another to make sure that you have the system:
Take 37:

37 + 12 is 49. Reverse this and get 94
Now start off with 94 and the next digit is 3 (9 + 4 is 13)
Now you have 943
Now 3 + 4 is 7 and the next digit is 7
Now you have 9437
Now 7 + 3 is 10 and the next digit is 0
Now you have 94370

You can see that this can go indefinitely but you must carry
it out to only 10 places—which is plenty! You don't remember
the number, all you do is call off the digits one at a time.

In making up this list of 50 numbers don't have it consecutive. Have it all mixed up so that nobody will see the 31, 41, 51 etc. which is very noticeable when the numbers are in sequence.

A MORE DIFFICULT CARD TRICK

Slip the following four cards into your pocket unnoticed:

Ace of Spades
2 of Hearts
4 of Diamonds
8 of Clubs

Be sure that they are in this order so that when you put your hand in your pocket you will know that the Ace of Spades is the first card, the 2 of Hearts is the second card, etc.

Now have somebody shuffle the cards and cut the pack face down. Tell him to take a card from one of the two packs and show it to everyone and then put it back. After this has been done you take the other pack and, putting it in your pocket (carefully on top of the four cards that you already have there), ask what the card was. When you hear the card you put your hand into your pocket (where everyone saw you put the other half of the pack) and pull out a card of the same suit as the selected card. Now tell everyone that you will pull out another card or two more cards which will add up to the card selected. This you do to the astonishment of the crowd!

Here is what you do: Remembering that the combinations of 1, 2, 4 and 8 will make any number up to 13 (King) and knowing just where these cards are in your pocket as just described, all you need do is a little mental arithmetic. Suppose the card selected is the 9 of Hearts. You know right away that the second card in order in your pocket is a Heart (the 2 of Hearts) so you pull out the second card and say, "That's your suit." Now all you need do is add 1 and 8 to get 9 so the next two cards that you pull out of your pocket will be the Ace of Spades and the 8 of Clubs and these will add up to 9! Do this and say, "That adds up to your card."

In spite of the fact that half the shuffled pack is in your pocket and you have *called everyone's attention to this fact*, this does not interfere with the four original cards which are on the bottom, in the order named. Suppose the card chosen is the 5 of Spades. You first bring out the Ace (the bottom card in your pocket) and say, "That's your suit." Now go to the third card and bring out the 4 of Diamonds which, with the Ace will add to 5!

Don't do this trick more than twice in one evening. Learn it and practice it before you attempt it.

EASY WHEN YOU KNOW HOW

Without anyone seeing you, remove the following four cards from a pack: 2, Ace, 7, and 8. Put these on the top of the pack so that the 2 is the top card, the Ace is the next, the 7 is the next and the 8 is the fourth card. You realize, of course, that you can shuffle this pack without disturbing these four top cards, provided you shuffle them in your hands instead of in two piles, as is usual.

Shuffle the cards in this manner and select someone from the crowd. Tell him to take a number between 100 and 1000. There must be no zeros in the number, no repetition of digits, and the difference between the first and the last digit must be greater than 1—172, for example, does not count because the difference between 1 and 2 is not greater than 1. This leaves a wide range of numbers to choose from.

After he has selected his number, he must reverse the first and last digit—if he took 219 he must write 912, if he took 378 he must write 873, etc., and subtract one from the other. Now he must take the lesser from the greater, and he will get a new number in three digits. Tell him now to do the same thing with this new number, only instead of subtracting, add. For example, if his new number is 479, he is to add 974. As soon as he gets his answer, tell him to multiply it by 2. Here is the way he does it:

Suppose he took 874:

He writes down 874, and under it writes 478, thus   874
                                                     478

He takes one from the other and gets   396
Now he reverses 396 and gets 693.
He adds 693 to 396   1089
He now multiplies this by 2 and gets 2178.

No matter what numbers he takes, provided they obey the rules in the second paragraph, he will always get 2178.

Now, you merely tell the crowd that the first four cards you turn over will be this number. And, much to the astonishment of all, they are!

MORE THAN A COINCIDENCE

This startling trick is done with three coins: a half dollar, a quarter and a penny. It must be done by two people who know the code.

The first person (a man) leaves the room and everyone agrees on a number between 1 and 150. The man is called back and the girl (the other person who knows the trick) places the three coins on the back of a magazine for the man to look at. He looks at them and tells the number selected!

The trick is extremely simple. The magazine on which the coins are placed really represents an imaginary clock. With this in mind remember that whatever number the half dollar is on must be squared. Whatever number the quarter is on must be added to this (if heads) and subtracted (if tails). The penny is merely used to confuse the audience. It has no meaning at all.

Suppose the number selected were 86. The nearest square to 86 is 9 so the half dollar is placed where the 9 on the imaginary clock would be. Now we must add 5 to this so the quarter is placed on the 5 of the imaginary clock (heads up). The penny may be placed anywhere as it doesn't count.

Suppose 97 were chosen. 97 is really 10 squared minus 3, hence the half dollar goes on 10 and the quarter goes on 3 (tails up).

If the number chosen is a perfect square put the quarter on top of the half dollar and put both coins on the square root of the number. If it is 49 put both coins on 7, if it is 64 put both coins on 8, etc.

Suppose the number 2 is taken. 2 is really 2 squared minus 2. The half dollar goes on 2 and the quarter below it (toward the center of the clock) so that both coins are next to one another and the quarter is tails up. A better way to show this would be 3 squared minus 7. The half dollar on 3 and the quarter (tails up) on 7.

If negative numbers are chosen turn the half dollar tails up. No fractions are allowed.

A GOOD NUMBER TRICK

On a piece of paper write down any number between 1 and 50. Now fold the paper and give it to one of the guests in the room to hold, without looking at it. If you give it to a boy, tell him to put it in his pocket.

Now select anyone in the room and ask him to take a number between 50 and 100, without letting you see it. When he has done this, tell him to add to the number he has taken another number which you will give him. When he has done that tell him that he will have a number between 100 and 200 and he will agree with you. Now tell him to cross off the left digit of this number, which is 1, and add it to the remaining digits— if, for example, he has 135, he is to cross off the 1, add it to the 35 and get 36. As soon as he has done that, tell him to subtract this from his original number and watch the fun when you tell the boy to whom you gave the slip of paper to open it up. The numbers will agree!

This is how it is done:

The number that you tell your friend to add is always 99 minus the number you wrote on the paper. Be sure to remember this as it is very important. If you wrote 43 on the paper, you must tell him to add 56. If you wrote 34 on the paper, you must tell him to add 65.

Here is what happens behind the scenes:

What You Do	What Your Friend Does	
1. You write down any number less than 99 (say 23) on a piece of paper; fold it, and hand it to your friend, telling him not to look at it.	He slips the paper into his pocket without looking at it.	
2. Tell him to write down any number between 50 and 100 without letting you see it.	He writes 86.	
3. You subtract the number you wrote on the piece of paper (23) from 99 mentally, and tell your friend to add 76 to his number.	He adds:	86 76
		———
		162
4. Tell him to cross off the first number and add it to the result.	He does so:	X62 1
		———
		63
5. Now tell him to subtract his result from the original number and look at the folded piece of paper you gave him.	He subtracts:	86 63
		———
		23

CRAZY BETS—JUST FOR FUN

Try these on your friends.

1. I bet I can put myself through a key hole! (Write "myself" on a piece of paper and put it through the key hole)

2. I bet I can jump across the street! (Go across the street and then jump)

3. I bet I have something outside that will go out when it comes in! (Bring in a flashlight and let it go out when it comes in)

4. I bet I have a piece of paper in my pocket with some handwriting on it that you will want to pay me 95¢ for! (Take out a dollar bill and show the signature of the Treasurer, etc.)

5. I bet I have more money in my pocket than you have no matter how much you have! (Sure you have, since *his* money is not in *your* pocket)

6. I bet you use something every day that doesn't belong to you! (The alphabet or numbers)

7. I bet I can stand less than an inch away from you and you won't be able to touch me! (Stand on the other side of a door so that the door is between you and your friend)

8. I bet I can write a much longer word than you can no matter what word you write! (Write, "a much longer word than you can")

9. I bet I can pick something off the table without touching it! (Use a magnet and pick up a tack)
10. I bet you can't take off your coat alone! (As soon as he does this, start to take off your coat, too)

11. I bet you can't answer four questions wrong! (Ask three questions which he will answer wrong, then pause and say in an offhand manner, "Let me see . . . that's three, isn't it?" and he will say, "yes," which is the correct answer)

MIND READING STUNTS

THE MYSTERY OF MIND READING

Even if people realize that there is some trick to "mind reading," they still want to be mystified. It keeps them guessing—and they love it! First, they are completely baffled, then the light seems to dawn and they are sure they know just how it is done . . . then they find that they are all wrong—and they cry for more! This makes "mind reading" one of the most popular forms of family and party entertainment and one without which no gathering is complete.

Any one "mind reading" stunt may be repeated as often as your guests want it repeated. The fun is in trying to guess how you do it—and in many cases you will have to repeat it five or six times before anyone catches on. The Silent Telepathy stunt, however, should be performed only once in an evening.

Of course all of these stunts require the cooperation of a confederate who should be coached beforehand. As all of these stunts are ridiculously easy, your confederate will have no trouble at all in catching on and working with you all the way.

SILENT TELEPATHY

Send your confederate out of the room, instructing him that you are going to think of some person in the room whom he must name by "reading your thoughts." Of course, you have coached him in advance but nobody knows it. While he is out of the room everyone agrees on a particular person for you to "think about." Now you may call your confederate back. As soon as he enters the room everyone must be silent while you assume an attitude of deep thought and concentration. After a minute or less he will name the person you are thinking about, much to the astonishment of the crowd.

The code to this is so simple that it is laughable—yet nobody will get it right away. You, in your deep concentration, are sitting with your legs crossed and your shoe nonchalantly pointing to the chosen person. You have assumed this position before your confederate entered so you can be sure, even if you are not looking up, that your shoe is pointing correctly. Your confederate, of course, must not stare at your shoe. He should just glance at it when he enters and then assume an attitude of deep thought for at least 15 or 20 seconds to give the desired effect. Then he should name the person to whom your shoe points. After you are sure he has noticed your original position, you may change it.

If the person chosen is sitting next to you or is somewhere your shoe can't point without being obvious, the position of your *right arm* in your lap will do the trick and your legs, *not being crossed,* will tell your confederate to look at your right arm.

This may also be done by changing your position. You do not assume an attitude of deep concentration but just sit there silently, and let your confederate name the one who was chosen. In this case your posture is the same as that of the chosen person. If he has his right leg crossed over his left, you should have *your* right leg crossed over your left. If he is holding his cigarette a certain way, you should hold yours the same way—all without being obvious.

OAR

In this stunt three people are asked to stand next to each other while your confederate is out of the room. One of the three is chosen. Now your confederate is called back, and, *while you go out of the room and remain out of the room,* he names the chosen person! This is most mysterious since you are not in the room to give any kind of hidden clue and nobody has said a word. How does your confederate know the chosen person?

The code is just as simple as it can be. When you call your confederate in you say one of three things: O.K., Alright, or Ready. This spells the word OAR which he knows. If you said "O.K." he knows it is O and therefore the person on the left as he faces the three. If you said "Alright" he knows that it is A or the person in the middle, and, if you said "Ready" he knows that it is the person on the right—all according to the way these three letters appear in the word OAR. You don't have to be present after you say one of these three appropriate and totally "unsuspectable" words—and of course you say the right word in the most offhand and nonchalant manner. To make the stunt more baffling be sure to go out of the room *before* your confederate comes in so that he won't see you.

NAMING THE CORRECT CARD

Nine cards are placed on the floor—face up—in three rows of three cards each. While your confederate is out of the room someone selects a card. Your confederate will name it when he returns without your saying a word!

Any one of the following three codes will accomplish this and baffle everyone at the party. Here are the codes:

CODE 1

Pretend to read a magazine. You don't need to look up and don't need to say a word. Your unnoticed thumb on the cover of the magazine will give the location of the card on the floor. If your thumb is at the *upper left-hand corner of the magazine cover,* the selected card is the first one (the one at the *upper left-hand corner*). If your thumb is right *in the middle of the magazine cover*, then the selected card is then *the middle card*.

Your confederate should just glance at your thumb in relation to the magazine cover and then not look at it again. He should *not* look at your thumb the instant he comes in—it might look suspicious.

CODE 2

The room represents the rectangle of the nine cards as they are laid out on the floor. It is an easy matter to stand or sit in the part of the room represented by the selected card in the rectangle. If the selected card is the last one (the lower right-hand card), you will sit or stand in the lower right-hand part of the room. If the card is the middle card, stand in the middle of the room. Both you and your confederate should mentally divide the room into nine squares, the way the cards are divided, and you should be in the equivalent square of the chosen card.

CODE 3

This requires a little advance memory work—but it's worth it. Take the word OAR again. The O is the first row, the A the second row and the R the last row. The O, A and R are the positions of the cards in each row.

We then have a system just like the previous stunt only we use letters instead of numbers. O-O would be the first card in the first row; O-A the second card in the first row, and O-R the third card in the first row.

A-O is the first card in the second row, A-A the second card in the second row and A-R the third card in the second row. R-O is the first card in the third row, R-A is the second card in the third row and R-R is the last card in the third row.

Say to your confederate in the next room "O.K.—Alright" and he knows that it is O-A or the second card in the first row. Or say "Right—O.K." and he knows that it is R-O or the first card in the third row. Always give him two words of the OAR combinations and he can work it out in the other room. You can then leave the room before he enters and he will select the chosen card all by himself, much to the amazement of everybody!

TELEPATHY WITH QUESTIONS

In doing these stunts be sure to tell everyone that you have a confederate who is working with you. It is up to the audience to discover the code and you may repeat the stunt as often as you want, letting everyone try to discover your secret.

Your confederate leaves the room and any state in the United States is named. When he comes back you name state after state; when you finally name the chosen state he will say, "Yes." Here is how it works:

Suppose you choose New York. Your confederate comes back and you ask him, "Is it Idaho?" He will say, "No." "Is it Mississippi?" you ask. He will say, "No." You keep this up until you decide to ask, "Is it New York?" and he will say, "Yes."

The code is very simple. The chosen state is always named third after a state with a girl's name. The states that have girls' names are Delaware (Della), Maryland (Mary), Virginia and West Virginia, North and South Carolina (Caroline), Louisiana (Louise), Minnesota (Minna) and Idaho (Ida).

Here is a typical question: (The state is New York.)

YOU: "Is it Montana?"
HE: "No."
YOU: "Is it Oregon?"
HE: "No."
YOU: "Is it Virginia?"
HE (*noting the girl's name state*): "No"
YOU: "Is it Utah?
HE: "No." (This is the first state after the girl's name state.)
YOU: "Is it Pennsylvania?"
HE: "No." (This is the second state after the girl's name state)
YOU: "Is it New York?"
HE: "Yes." (This is the *third* state after the girl's name state.)

Note that it makes no difference how many girl's name states are mentioned after the first one nor does it matter if the chosen state is a girl's name state. The code is: The third state named after the first state whose name is that of a girl.

PSYCHIC QUESTIONS

This is a splendid trick which must not be done with less than eight people.

Have everyone in the room write a question which he wants answered. Now all papers are folded several times and dropped into a hat that you pass around.

Now seat yourself at a table at one end of the room with your guests at the other end, and, with the hat of folded papers on the table in front of you and a trash basket handy, start your psychic reading.

Pull out one of the folded pieces of paper and, without unfolding it, hold it against your head and pretend to read the question "mentally," giving either a sensible or a foolish answer. As soon as you have done this open up the paper and read what is written on it. Now scramble the paper up and throw it in the basket and choose another paper from the hat and, without opening it go through the same performance all over again reading the question "mentally" and answering it. Continue this until nearly all of the questions have been answered, much to the astonishment of everyone.

Unless you have tried this trick you have no idea what an effect it produces. It looks exactly as though you had psychic powers and could read through the papers—but don't do the trick more than once in an evening. Here is the way it works:

Everyone has written a question and there are as many questions in the hat as there are people playing. Because there are more than eight people doing this trick the first question will go unnoticed. It is really the only fake question and you must make it up. It does not belong to anyone in the room and, since you don't call attention to it, each person will think it is someone else's question and it will go unnoticed. After you have "mentally" read and answered this fake question, open the paper and read the real question which is written on it to yourself, then scramble the paper up and throw it away. From now on it is very easy. To each paper that you pull out of the hat and hold against your forehead you apply the question which you read on the previous paper and it is impossible to tell the difference! As you finish "mentally" reading each question, answering it and asking the person who wrote it to stand up and verify it, you "check up" on your own psychic powers by opening up this question and "seeing if you were correct." Of course what you are really doing is reading the question which you must answer next but nobody realizes it.

You are always one jump behind the next paper but nobody knows it and, since you throw all these papers away there is no way of finding out. The only part of this trick to be careful about is the first question which you must make up yourself.

GAMES FOR THE
VERY YOUNG

TONGUE TWISTERS

Say each of these as quickly as you can.

Round and round the rugged rocks the ragged rascal ran.

Betty Botta bought a bit o' butter. "But," said she, "This butter's bitter. If I put it in my batter it will make my batter bitter." So Betty Botta bought a bit o' butter and put it in her bitter batter which made Betty Botta's bitter batter a bit better.

Theyssian Thyssel is a successful thistle sifter. He sifts sieves full of three thousand thistles through the thick of his thumb. If those thistle sifters who sift sieves of thistles think of Theyssian Thyssel, the successful thistle sifter, they will be successful at sifting thistle sieves.

Peter Pepper picked a peck of pickled peppers. A peck of pickled peppers Peter Pepper picked. If Peter Pepper picked a peck of pickled peppers, where's the peck of pickled peppers Peter Piper picked?

Bill Bord had a board bill and a billboard. Both the board bill and the billboard bored Bill Bord. So Bill Bord sold the billboard to pay his board bill and now neither the board bill nor the billboard will bore Bill Bord.

Say "Bad Blood" ten times very quickly.

She's so selfish she should sell shellfish, but shellfish shells seldom sell.

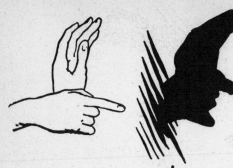

WHAT A NOSE !

THE REINDEER

BUTTERFLY

THE WOLF

A NATIVE PRINCE

THE GOOSE

THE OLD MAN ENJOYS A SMOKE

IS THIS THE WINNER? —

HOLIDAY FUN

SHADOWGRAPHS

Shadowgraphs are loads of fun to make—when you know how. And the nicest thing about them is that you don't need any lessons to learn how . . . you just hold your two hands in different ways, with a candle in front of them and a white wall or sheet behind them, and you will see all the fine animals and odd-shaped creatures pictured on the following pages.

Have the room dark except for one candle. Have a light wall or a sheet about three feet from the candle and hold your hands between the candle and the wall or sheet. Try to copy each of the pictures shown here and see how the shadow springs to life. It's easy to do and a lot of fun!

FUNNY PICTURES

Give each boy and girl a pencil and a strip of paper about two inches wide and ten or twelve inches long. Each player must start by drawing the funniest face he or she can, leaving two lines for the neck and folding the paper over so that nothing can be seen other than the two projecting neck lines. The papers are then passed and the funniest body is put on to this neck. The legs are not to be drawn, just the body. Four guide lines for the two legs are to be put in at the bottom of the body so that the next player will know where to put the legs. Papers are then folded until only these four guide lines are showing, and passed. Now the legs are to be drawn in, but *not* the feet. Everything goes the same as before—the papers are folded and passed —and the last things to be put in are the feet. These should also be as funny as you can make them. When all this has been done, the papers are unfolded and some mighty crazy-looking pictures will be seen.

This game can also be done with animals instead of persons, thus a dog's head and a pig's body, etc., are drawn.

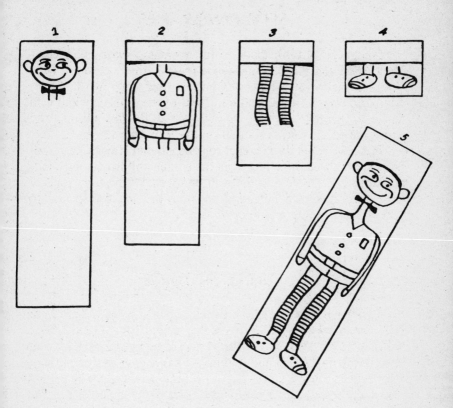

THE PYRAMID

The seven letters below will make seven different words. Start by putting a one letter word in the top box. Under it put a two letter word, using the letter in the top box as one of the letters. Under this put a three letter word, using both the letters of the two letter word. Keep this up, always using the letters of the previous word and adding one letter to form the next word, until you reach the bottom with a seven letter word. Use only the letters given. Several players will have different words. One suggested answer is given at the end of this section.

ALPHABET OBJECTS

There are 26 objects here. Each one starts with a letter of the alphabet, one with A, one with B, and so on. How quickly can you write the names of all these objects in alphabetical order? You may look at the picture as often as you wish but be sure to get all 26. And do it in the shortest possible time. Answer is given at the end of this section.

OPTICAL ILLUSIONS

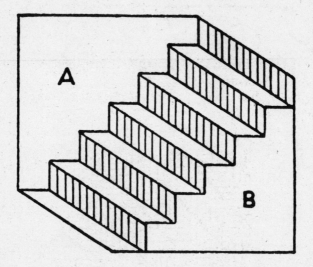

Is A the nearer wall of this staircase or is it B? Look closely and watch the one give place to the other.

A appears to be higher than its width.

B appears to be a rectangle whose width is greater than its height.

Is this so? No. Both A and B are perfect squares.

The divided line BC appears to be longer than AB, but they are exactly the same length.

In spite of their apparent waywardness, these diagonal lines are actually parallel.

Here is an amusing little test in gauging distance. How does the distance between points A and B compare with the distance between points B and C?

Despite appearances, the upright lines are both parallel and straight.

Here are two strips, A and B, cut from a circle. How do you think they compare in size? Test them and see.

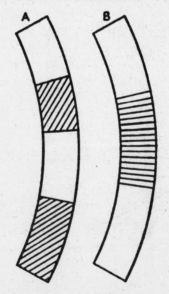

TOY STORE OBSERVATION

The drawing below shows a toy store. As you can see, there are two windows, one for boys and the other for girls. Look at the picture very carefully for about three minutes. Then, with-

out looking at this page, see how many of the objects shown here you can remember. The time limit for your answers is five minutes.

BOXES

This is a game for two or more, but it is best when played by only two players.

Make a series of dots as indicated in the diagram. Each player takes a turn in connecting two dots with a line. The object is to make as many squares (or boxes) as you can and at the same time prevent the other player from making squares or boxes. As the game progresses there will be a time when one of the players must get a box or two boxes or three boxes, and that is when it gets exciting.

A player may only make a box when the other three sides have been made. If there are a number of three sided squares, the same player may complete all these squares for boxes. This is shown in the diagram. As soon as a player has made a box he puts his initial in it; the one having the most boxes wins. The number of boxes possible, of course, depends on the number of dots, which must always make a square.

HANGMAN

This is one of the most popular games played with pencil and paper. It should be played by two people, one choosing a word and the other trying to guess the word chosen. Suppose you and I play the game. I take a word and put down as many dashes as there are letters in the word. If there are five letters in the word I will put down five dashes. Above these dashes I write the alphabet and over to the left of the paper I make a little gallows to "hang" you with. It is now up to you to guess the letters in my word; for each wrong letter I add a new part of your body to the gallows. Each letter that is guessed I cross out in the alphabet so that it won't be guessed again. Each correct letter is put in its right place in the word. You must guess the word before you are completely "hanged." The figure shows you just what the paper should look like.

Suppose I choose the word CANDY. I make five dashes as shown. Suppose you guess the letter J. I cross off J in the alphabet and give you a head on the gallows (just a circle) because there is no J in CANDY. You then guess the letter B. I cross off B in the alphabet and put one eye in your head because there is no B in CANDY. Each time you guess a letter that is not in the word I add something to your body as you hang from the gallows. Each correct letter is put in its place in the dashed word. It is up to you to guess the right letters of the word before I "hang" you.

MAKING A MOTOR BOAT

Take the top of a cigar box and cut it out as shown below. Place a rubber band around the two notches on the boat, as indicated, and twist the propeller round and round to "wind it up." Watch the boat go when you release it in a tub of water!

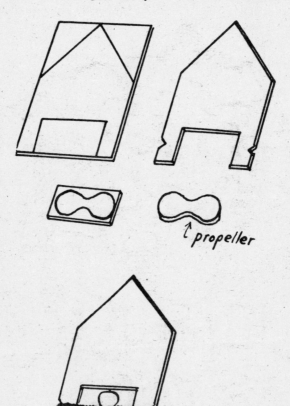

propeller

rubber band

HOW MANY FACES?

My, what a lot of faces there are! About twenty of them can be found in a few minutes. Put a number on every nose. That is one way to determine the number of faces you have found—by counting noses!

BIRD BRAINS

These poor headless birds are all numbered as you can see. Can you put the number of the bird next to the head you think it fits, in the space where all the heads are drawn? Perhaps you can even go a step farther and copy the proper heads on the birds themselves. Answer is given at the end of this section.

Here they are: can you number them correctly?

24 MINUS 8 EQUALS 2

Place 24 matches in the position shown below to form nine squares. Can you remove only eight matches and leave only two squares? Answer is given at the end of this section.

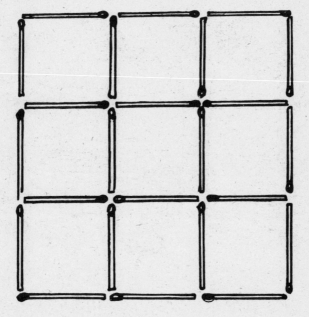

"B" ON THE LOOKOUT

There are fifty-six objects beginning with B in this picture. How many can you find? The first player to write down fifty on a sheet of paper wins. If there is a tie, look for the other six objects. If you put down anything you do not actually see in the picture it counts against you and you may lose the game when the lists are compared. Answers are given at the end of this section.

CUTTING THE WALLS

The diagram below represents 15 walls. Draw a continuous line through each of the walls without ever going through any wall twice. Answer is given at the end of this section.

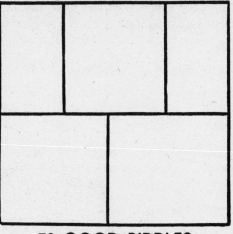

70 GOOD RIDDLES

Try them on your friends.

1. What is it that dogs have that nothing else has? *Puppies.*

2. Take two letters from a five letter word and have one left. *Take s and t from stone and have one.*

3. When does a farmer have the best chance to see his pigs? *When he has a sty in his eye.*

4. When is the only time a man is really immersed in his business? *When he is giving a swimming lesson.*

5. What lives in winter, dies in summer and grows with its roots upwards? *An icicle.*

6. What is most like a hen stealin'? *A cock robin.*

7. What men are the most above board? *Chessmen.*

8. What contains more feet in winter than in summer? *An outdoor skating rink.*

9. What is the best way to keep water from coming into your house? *Don't pay your water tax.*

10. A man bought two fishes but had three when he got home. Explain this. *He had two fishes—and one smelt.*

11. On which side of a church does a cypress tree grow? *The outside.*

12. Why is the letter A like a honeysuckle? *A B always follows it.*

13. Why is O the noisiest vowel? *All other vowels are inaudible.*

14. Why does a blow leave a blue mark when it is over? *Because the past of blow is blew.*

15. What does a girl look for that she doesn't want to find? *A run in her stocking.*

16. What relation is the doormat to the doorstop? *Step-father.*

17. What will be yesterday tomorrow and was tomorrow yesterday? *Today.*

18. What gets bigger the more you contract it? *A debt.*

19. When is vegetable soup sure to run out of the soup plate? *When there's a leek in it.*

20. What kind of hen lays the longest? *A dead one.*

21. When can a woman be said to be head over ears in debt? *When she hasn't paid for the wig she's wearing.*

22. What is the difference between 16 ounces of lead and a pianist? *The pianist pounds away and the lead weighs a pound.*

23. Why is ink like a pig? *Because they both stay in a pen.*

24. Which takes the least time to get ready for a trip: An elephant or a rooster? *The cock. He only takes his comb while the elephant has to take a whole trunk.*

25. Why is the letter D like a bad boy? *Because it makes ma mad.*

26. Why is the letter E always grouchy? *Because, while it is never out of health or pocket, it never appears in good spirits.*

27. What is the difference between a well-dressed man and a tired dog? *The man wears an entire suit while the tired dog just pants.*

28. When is a soldier charitable? *When he presents arms.*

29. What is the difference between a jeweler and a jailer? *One sells watches and other watches cells.*

30. What occurs once in a minute, twice in a moment and not at all in a hundred thousand years? *The letter M.*

31. How would you swallow a door? *Bolt it.*

32. When does a chair hate you? *When it can't bear you.*

33. It belongs to you yet your friends, without buying, borrowing or stealing it, use it much more than you do. What is it? *Your name.*

34. Why can't we fight with actresses? *They make up too quickly.*

35. What does no man want yet no man wants to lose? *A bald head.*

36. What is the difference between a beautiful girl and a mouse? *A mouse harms the cheese; the girl charms the he's.*

37. Why is a man who is always complaining the easiest man to satisfy? *Because nothing satisfies him.*

38. Where are you sure to go when you are twelve years old? *Into your thirteenth year.*

39. Which is correct: "the white of the eggs *is* yellow," or "the white of the eggs *are* yellow?" *Neither. White is never yellow.*

40. Which candles burn longer: wax candles or tallow candles? *Neither. They both burn shorter.*

41. What speaks every language? *An echo.*

42. Why can't it rain for two days continually? *Because there is always a night in between.*

43. If eight crows are on a roof and you shoot one, how many remain? *None. They all fly away.*

44. How can five people divide five cookies so that each gets a cookie and yet one cookie remains on the plate? *The last person takes the plate along with the cookie.*

45. What question can never be answered by "yes"? *"Are you asleep?"*

46. What is full of holes yet holds water? *A sponge.*

47. Four fat women were under one small umbrella during a terrible storm. Why didn't they get wet? *It was a sand storm.*

48. What is the longest word in the English language? *Smiles. There is a mile between the first and last letters.*

49. What is the only thing you break when you say its name? *Silence.*

50. What is bought by the yard yet worn by the foot? *Carpet.*

51. What horse sees as much in the rear as he does in the front? *A blind horse.*

52. How many peas go into one pot? *None. You have to put them in the pot.*

53. How far can you go into the woods? *As far as the center.
From then on you will be going out of the woods.*

54. What bird looks most like the stork? *The stork's wife.*

55. What's the best way to carry water in a sieve? *Freeze the
water first.*

56. If a telephone and a piece of paper had a race, who would
win? *The telephone since the paper will always remain
stationary.*

57. Why does an Indian wear feathers in his hair? *To keep
his wig warm.*

58. Why is a man who doesn't place bets at the races just as
bad as one who does?" *Because he is no better.*

59. If you saw a counterfeit bill on the sidewalk and walked
by without picking it up, why would you be arrested? *Because you are passing counterfeit money.*

60. In a certain word the letter L is in the middle, in the beginning and at the end. There is only one L in the word. What
is the word? *The word is "inland." L is in the middle. In is
at the beginning. And is at the end.*

61. Why is the nose in the middle of the face? *Because it is a
scenter.*

62. What will go up a chimney down but will not go down a
chimney up? *An umbrella.*

63. What goes from New York to Chicago without moving an
inch? *The road.*

64. Why is a caterpillar like a hot biscuit? *Because it makes
the butterfly.*

65. What is the difference between a cloud and a spanked
boy? *A cloud pours with rain and a spanked boy roars
with pain.*

66. What is the difference between a man going up a staircase and a man looking up a staircase? *One is stepping up stairs and the other staring up steps.*

67. What is the difference between an old penny and a new dime? *Nine cents.*

68. Why is Ireland the wealthiest country? *Because its capital is always Dublin.*

69. What is the difference between a cat and a comma? *The cat has claws at the end of paws; the comma is a pause at the end of a clause.*

70. Why should fish be well educated? *They are found in schools.*

ANSWERS

THE PYRAMID

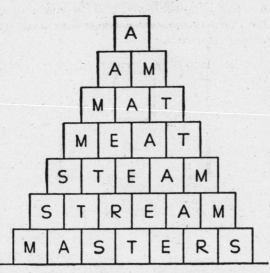

ALPHABET OBJECTS

A—Anchor
B—Book
C—Cat
D—Daisy
E—Egg
F—Fish
G—Grapes
H—Hat
I—Ink

J—Jam
K—Kite
L—Lamp
M—Mouse
N—Needle
O—Owl
P—Pear
Q—Question Mark
R—Rabbit

S—Snake
T—Table
U—Umbrella
V—Vase
W—Wheel
X—Xylophone
Y—Yacht
Z—Zebra

BIRD BRAINS

24 MINUS 8 EQUALS 2

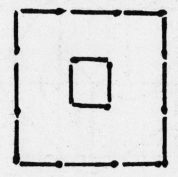

"B" ON THE LOOKOUT

Baby	Basket	Billboard
Bacon	Bat	Bi-plane
Bakery	Bathers	Birds
Balcony	Bath house	Blinds
Bald-headed man	Bathing suit	Boarding house
Ball	Bay	Boards
Balloon	Bay window	Boat
Balistrade	Beach	Book
Bank	Beacon	Boots
Banana	Beads	Bottles
Banners	Beard	Bow
Barn	Beans	Box
Barber shop	Beef	Boy
Barrel	Belt	Brackets

Bracelet	Bridge	Butcher
Braids	Bull dog	Butterflies
Bread	Buns	Buttons
Branch	Bundle	Bushes
Bricks	Buoy	

CUTTING THE WALLS

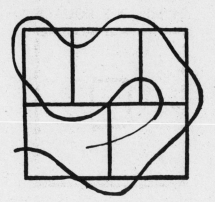